PIERRE
DROULERS
CHOREOGRAPHER

sun day

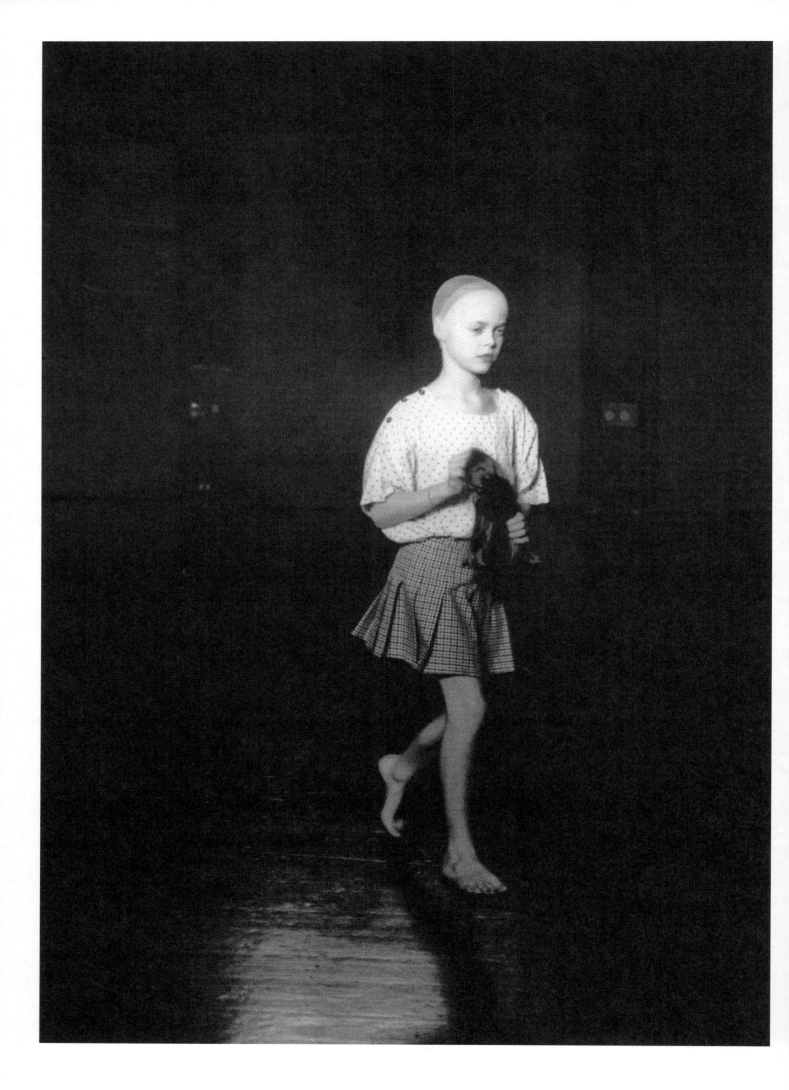

PIERRE
DROULERS
CHOREOGRAPHER

sun day

EDITED BY PIERRE DROULERS

CHARLEROI DANSES
MERCATORFONDS

distributed by
YALE UNIVERSITY PRESS
New Haven and London

EUGÈNE   SAVITZKAYA

FOR THE METICULOUS CHOREOGRAPHER

Innocent, the body jumps and, before
jumping, sleeps and, before sleeping,
breathes and, before breathing, feeds
using up the good reserves, using its
life in dance, in the movement of
arms and legs, of the head and the
trunk along the axis of the shin,
the shoulders and the wrists and the
kneecaps and the fingers and the toes
softened by walking on the stripped
earth, flexing the joints, stretching
the tendons, breathing the
surrounding air like we taste wine
and the precious roots, breathing
out over and over again the breath
warmed by the liquid circulating
in intimate vessels, sweating blood
and water, the brain clear like a
pure container, wavy hair, skin in
direct contact with the ground, this
drum skin and drum with an earthly
resonance.

But dancing, don't forget anything,
not the whale-shaped cloud that
clings to the hill nor the wave
that lifts up the vessel, the sternum
stretched like a wishbone with
its little piece of gristle that

disturbs the sun, neither apophysis
nor symphysis, nor the movement of
the stars, nor the wear and tear of
the fabric.

Free-hipped, the body turns and the
skeleton moves under a shower of red
sand, under pollen grain dust, and
the dragon's shadow is projected on
the barbed-wired horizon of the sea.
The organism thus adopts the crab's
walk, the spider's or the fly's, the
bottom becoming the top, and the top
the bottom. And the universe is held
in a pebble that sculpts the currents
and the ocean swell.

The body is the one that sends
the waves over the innocent surface
worked by the underground tides,
forwards and backwards, and
backwards and forwards, depending
on the coming and going of life, of
copulation, of backwash, of tectonic
friction.

The bird rows and the human being
paddles. But the flower sways.

The Light at the Beginning

Material Dreams

Conflagration

THE BODY AT WORK

PROLOGUE

There. There we are.

The body of the poem is dismembered.

On the second floor of La Raffinerie, in what has become the Brussels home for Charleroi Danses, twenty-five tables have been set out.

Dissecting tables, anatomy of a choreographer's work, a jumbled archive (photographs, various texts, recordings, objects), fragments of a dispersed memory, waiting for the gesture that will unite them, strip them down, distil them.

The resources are there. It could end up as a complete catalogue, arranged and organised as it should be.

But no. Unfolding the past, certainly, but to find it, between storms and calmer landscapes, bodies that have been resuscitated. A tree-like lifeblood. An underlying beating.

What the excavations uncover, the present organises. And so, the ghostly bodies come back to life, animated by a rhythm that seems bit by bit, by successive clarifications, to find its internal logic. The film of a life and many other lives.

On stage, there was jostling. Such a face encapsulates a whole body of stories. Such a landscape seems to be still inhabited with the atmospheres that brought it to life. Pierre Droulers' process of choreographic composition is made up of sampling, gatherings, frictions, agitated moments, finding here a restarted organicity, creating a layout that retains the form of a sort of staging.

Is it an exaggeration to say that this book is a new work by the poet-choreographer, an embodiment of material that memory seems have rendered speechless, caught in the moment of a snapshot or in the recording of a document, but in a crowded, noisy, amazingly animated silence?

A body of work, in other words, that remembers and is nourished by multifarious bodies: physical, musical, literary, whether intimate or ample.

A journey.

CHILDHOOD

Childhood, what is the essence?

First of all, there is the house in the north, 'a large house in a town with three small adjoining gardens'. Not really family life as we usually know it, but an artistic atmosphere: painting lessons every Monday, museum visits on Sunday, a never-ending flow of painter and sculptor friends. An openness to the outside, with African students invited every week. And a hint of spirituality: services with all religions mixed up, and discussions about Jiddu Krishnamurti's thinking. 'Dad had this taste for the minimal, for the almost nothing, for the ephemeral.' For performance, as well, judging by the photo of the little puppet theatre made by the father, Robert/Roberto.

When he was thirteen, Droulers was sent south. Avignon, Lycée Saint Joseph, run by the Jesuits. The pictures are missing.

DANCING/EXPERIMENTING

Is there a first memory of dance? Yes, maybe. End of the secondary-school years. With the senior brother, a Merce Cunningham performance in Saint-Paul-de-Vence. A sparse crowd. What remains in the memory? A gesture. The hand waving to the dancers as they left on board a coach.

It's certainly not enough to encourage the story of a calling.

With his studies successfully completed, Droulers allowed himself to take a year off, 'I said that I wanted to dance, I don't really know why I said that.' 'He's not yet trained, but he's got a good plié, he can adapt,' proclaimed Serge Golovine. Pliés, jetés, the whole kit and caboodle: off to Rosella Hightower's dance school in Cannes. Body training. Here as well, the pictures are missing. Instead, another parallel existence immersed in the energy of a punk group, Peet and Ses Rats. Rimbaud not far off?

And then Mudra, Brussels. Maurice Béjart opens his school in an old tramway shed. The inaugural class. 'There was no background history, no earlier generation, the atmosphere was completely pure.' Béjart dreamed of total art, 'everything we were taught was new', but Béjart no doubt thought more about hiring from among the Mudra students to build up his own company.

Except it was not long before Béjart was marginalised because of a certain conventionalism. In Brussels, Théâtre 140, directed by Jo Dekmine, an insatiable talent spotter, put on all kinds of mad shows: Living Theatre, Jerzy Grotowski, the Londoners from the People Show, Johnny Rotten, and so on… And Paris was not so far away. Putting everything else aside, there was only one reason to go to Paris: a certain Bob Wilson and the phenomenally leisurely pace of *Deafman Glance*, followed a year later, in 1972, by *Overture* (continuous 24-hour performance) at the Opéra Comique, as part of the first Festival d'Automne. Astonishing, 'this completely unexpected notion

1   'Traversée', working document, transcribed by Marion Rhéty, 2011.

---

of space-time', the 'physical beauty behind which we felt all the work done
back in the studio', but also the diversity of Bob Wilson's performers,
including the autistic participants such as the extraordinary Christopher
Knowles.

We look in vain for the remains of a legacy. And yet, with Bob Wilson,
there was also a sense of initiation: 'at Mudra, all that gave us ideas to
experiment with all sorts of things'. In May 1976, as he was finishing his
training at Mudra, Droulers created his first performance at Théâtre 140.
Désert was, says the performance programme, 'A piece that was half dance,
half theatre, where the words, a blend of cries and singing, encounter
the bodies in movement head-on; wrestling with space, bodies on bodies,
hazardous walks in successive orbits, where sweat, blood and sand spurt into
the overheated air.' Today, Droulers remembers: 'There were three or four
of us walking about, and other people were circling around us as if we were
prisoners.' No working method: 'I worked by instinct, by intuition.'[1]

The following year, *Dispersion*, with Diane Broman, Juliana Carneiro da
Cunha and Nicole Mossoux. 'Texts, sounds, movement, decorative metamorphoses
join in a game of ambiguous interventions between dream and reality,'
wrote André Drossart in *Le Soir*. All the sources of inspiration do not
necessarily appear on the surface. Or is it that they are already there,
but will spring up later? On one of the tables in La Raffinerie, spread
out around a few photos of *Dispersion*, are the faces of Arthur Rimbaud
and Johnny Rotten, striking side by side, a poster of the Art Ensemble
of Chicago, a book by the Italian dramatist Carmelo Bene, and the mention
of a poem by John Giorno, 'Grasping at Emptiness', taken from an issue of
Schizofrenia magazine, which used to be passed around from hand to hand
at Plan K (the previous incarnation of La Raffinerie).

A PERIOD OF THE PRESENT MOMENT

We are no doubt talking about a period when even the notion of a 'young
choreographer' had no meaning, because everything was incredibly young.
Free jazz and punk music, outlandish performances, jaunts to Paris to
go and pogo dance at Le Gibus, etc. Nothing was premeditated, everything
existed in the present, without putting together a file of documents for the
next piece, nor applications for subsidies. Droulers did, however, receive
a grant to go to New York, to complete his training as a 'dancer' at Merce
Cunningham's studio, which he abandoned as soon as he arrived. It was still
too conventional. His career path evolved through chance encounters: poets

2   Guy Duplat, *La Libre Belgique*, 11 and 12 May 2013.
3   Interview with Guy Duplat, *La Libre Belgique*, 7 May 2013.

---

of the Beat generation, jazz clubs, and Steve Paxton, who he discovered in St Mark's Church, performing as a duo with the percussionist David Moss. Let go, release. No doubt the pieces of work that followed the stay in New York – *Hedges* (1979), with the saxophonist-improviser Steve Lacy; *Tao* (1980), with the very Wilsonian Sheryl Sutton; *Tips* (1981), with François Hiffler and Pascale Murtin, the duettists from Grand Magasin; and *Pieces for Nothing* (1982), 'bursts of movement captured in full flight' with the musicians from the rock group Minimal Compact – would today be called 'performances'. Actually, labels hardly count. Happy is he who discovers them.

CHANGE OF SCENE, LIGHT

Far away from the cauldron of New York, talk about other journeys.
Beyond the line between Gare du Midi (Brussels) and Gare du Nord (Paris), look for a change of scene, the experience of being away from home. Wrocław, Poland, the year when Jerzy Grotowski opened up his theatre-laboratory to young 'westerners' for the first time. There again, the pictures are missing, apart from a photo of the 'master'. So we need to imagine the area of forests and lakes where the workshop was taking place, the mad races through the woods, an old cottage filled with bunches of mint, experiencing a physical exhaustion from which must emerge an actor's performance stripped of all desire for interpretation.
And Brazil (no pictures) on the trail of *Orfeu Negro*, the film shot by Marcel Camus in a Rio de Janeiro favela. And there, let yourself be guided and grabbed by the sound and the rhythm of the candomblé drums. Initiation into voodoo, in a trance, the spirits take form. The magic of ritual which, many years later, after marinating for a long time, resonates in 2013 in the creation of *Soleils*, a carnivalesque whirlwind of bodies that 'climaxes in a mad dance towards the sun and mystery'.[2] An exorcism. The solar energy of Brazil found a reply in the shadows cast by Japan (*Kyoto Experiment*, 2012). Droulers: 'I am fascinated by these two countries and by the contrasts that they embody. How does light react between these two polarities? What metamorphoses take place?'[3]
Europe too was bathing in nuances of light. The changing light of the North Sea, the Ostend jetty (*La Jetée*, 1983). An unresolved image, translucent, a waking dream. In the South, fragments from a stay in Italy, livelier colours, blues, orangey. '06.50 when the sun rose each colour subtly changing from one minute to the next then after a certain time (evidently) we stop looking.'[4]

4   Pierre Droulers, notebook, 5 August 1981.
5   Clara Van Campenhout, interview with Sofie Kokaj and Hans Theys, *Cahier MA*, nº9, p. 13.
6   'Traversée', working document, transcribed by Marion Rhéty, 2011.

From *La Jetée* onwards, from east to west and from north to south, it could
be tempting to retrace the steps through each Pierre Droulers work, like so
many stages of a sensorial journey that travels through changing states of
light, the *illuminations* (here we find Rimbaud) alternating with the dark
blackness, and always there would be a twilight zone (*Light No Light*, the
title of a film by Ludovica Riccardi on the work of a choreographer), like
an undefinable frontier where perceptions are mixed and confused, up to
the experience of the barrier of fog, attempted at the Centre de Création
Contemporaine in Tours, with Ann Veronica Janssens:'the stage flooded by an
artificial fog', the audience wandering around the stage, able to hear but
not to see.

SCORES, WRITINGS

On the tables on the second floor of La Raffinerie: notebooks, drawings,
plans and diagrams. Everything in a jumbled-up order. When working on
Comme si on était leurs petits poucets (1991), the final pages of James
Joyce's *Finnegans Wake* were cut up, line by line, and stuck on large pieces
of paper. For *De l'air et du vent* (1996), the eye is drawn to a group of A4
sheets, on which small sketched illustrations follow one after the other, a
sort of storyboard for the piece. But nothing is ever that simple. There is
a profusion of 'scores', and they are never the same, mixing up sources and
writings. And in any case, 'things are created through residues, what is
forgotten, what endures, and it can happen that the starting material can
be completely transformed, and can even quite simply disappear'.[5]
Quoting Walter Benjamin, Droulers likes to say that 'the labyrinth is the
homeland of he who hesitates'. Between chaos and form, for example. Working
in 'choreography' is not only (and sometimes, not at all) 'writing dance',
with a tangible architectural structure, duly constructed. For Droulers,
'dance is the way in which we connect with someone, to material, to sound. I
think more in terms of dream material than a mix of flowing frameworks. It's
the work of the dancer to link things and to put them into movement. What
is central to my work is, perhaps, not dance so much as movement. Like an
image appearing, disappearing… Everything is a pretext to join in the game
of harmony and disharmony.'[6]

DISTILLING

Working as a choreographer, or quite simply as an artist, is 'seeing how things are distilled'.

Literally, *La Distillerie de lavande*, a film shot by Droulers in Provence, close up to the movements of the maker who transforms the plant into scent.

Essence (look for the being rather than the doing) as a product of careful physical labour.

Even if, as the choreographer said in 1996, 'There are moments when I say to myself that maybe I must stop doing things and simply watch what is there.'[7]

A REPOSITORY

Final lap on the second floor of La Raffinerie, another final wander around the twenty-five tables set out there, on which is spread the repository of a life, the connecting threads of a life's work.

Silence, and unsteadiness.

Still unable to know how this exhibition of fragments will find its storyline within the pages of a book.

Gauging a certain powerlessness of words to translate and distil the numerous intensities that each document retains.

Winston Tong, the singer from Tuxedomoon; Stefan Dreher, the alter ego dancer; we must make a note of each name.

Behind each photographed face, the story of a meeting.

Behind each space (scenic or not), the memory of an escapade.

Behind each written page, excitement.

Here and there, the books. A double stamp of approval given straight away: Beckett and Joyce. Starkness, depreciation on one side; profusion, belligerence on the other. As if the work to come, today completed, never stopped navigating between these two poles.

And then, another viaticum: a small book with a silvery grey cover, *L'Homme des foules* (The Man of the Crowd) by Edgar Allan Poe, translated by Charles Baudelaire. And this is Droulers' approach to work, a stroll through the turmoil of the world, but a lively physical stroll, itself transfused by an impossible tranquillity. *Multum in Parvo* (1998), crowds and solitude, a communal performance woven from twenty-five solos, a collective herbarium of so many personal mythologies.

Beyond the finished, completed pieces, a memory remains of a work that

never saw the light of day, initially produced with and for Michael
Lonsdale. A free adaptation, under the title *Arriver/Partir*, of a poem by
Fernando Pessoa, 'Passagem das Horas', and of a text by Christian Dotremont,
'Digue'. A choir and a character, 'the man moving forward', who, with 'shoes
loaded with waves' and his 'suitcase full of diversions', tries to reach the
last open house, right at the end of the seawall.

From his earliest works, such as *Désert*, right up to his most recent
pieces, it's pleasing to think that Droulers is still captured by this
double movement of arriving (extracting from chaos some possible form) and
of leaving (distancing himself from form to go back and explore chaos),
without ever shutting himself away in the comfort of a 'style'. This book,
then, designed as a poetic creation, reassembling all the diversions
accumulated in his suitcases, waves removed from his shoes in order to
allow him to float away again, is that of a forward-moving artist, the body
working for an ever-changing state of being.

CHAPTER ONE

THE LIGHT AT THE BEGINNING

1951:   Pierre Droulers born in La Madeleine, Lille
1969-72:   Studies at Mudra in Brussels, dance school
           founded by Maurice Béjart
1971:   *Le Regard du sourd*, discovery of Robert Wilson in Paris
1976:   Creation of *Désert*, first performance piece

DÉSERT

Choreography: Pierre Droulers

With: Juliana Carneiro da Cunha, Danielle Cousins, Pierre Droulers, Jean Gaudin,

Jean-Christophe Lamy, Alain Louafi, Rachid Tika, Ahmid Tarqui

Music: Ricardo Castro

Text: Danielle Cousins, Pierre Droulers

Set design and costumes: Groupe Triangles

Lighting: Hubert Dombrecht

First performance: May 1976, Théâtre 140, Brussels

Filia

maison du nord   Mudra

la mère du nord

Bram
Droulers   papa   Pierre   magu
                      maman   Droulers   marin
                                                            Julian
              - concert punk à l'île d'yeu

tions

chambre à Bruxelles
le théâtre 140

"desert" 1976

le peo

TRIANGLES

Joe Dekmine

DESERT
1976

W. Burroughs

Maurice
Bejart
Jo
Dekmine
nerio
a cunha

OPENING BLUES.

She was naked,

no food on her lips,

no foot on her feet,

no paper on her skin,

only.. a star window,

running on back streets,

and many oceans ruling

on her beach body

sweet and sweet..

She was naked,

so sorry to be free...

Hot lifting the stairs of the last house,

Raining back on lips of time-apple,

She says, in a sigh of relief,

that she would like a sign,

a sign between us three..

She was naked !

She found a new way

of leaving the Earth...

Between the two worlds,

she cries a new song,

a BLUES BLUES BLUES,

which is so very true...

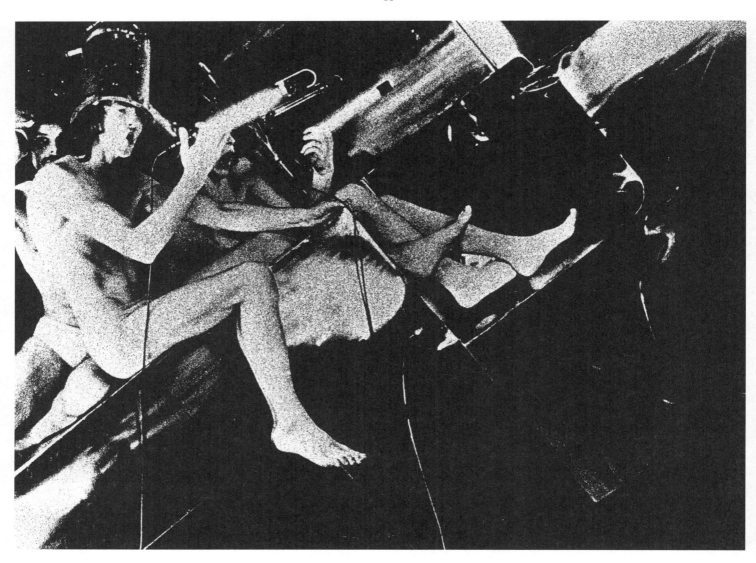

"The Penny Arcade Peep Show" d'après William Burroughs. Mise en scène : Frédéric Flamand. Acteurs : Baba, Bruno Garny, Frédéric Flamand. Structure mobile en acier inoxydable de Félix Roulin.

"The Penny Arcade Peep Show" évoque un univers de machines à sous, de quartiers mal famés, de luna-parks et de show pour spectateurs-voyeurs conviés à un voyage dans l'espace-temps. Les textes ont été choisis dans différents romans de W. S. Burroughs: "Le Festin Nu", "La Machine Molle", "Le Ticket qui explosa", "Nova Express" et "Les Garçons Sauvages". Un territoire au-devant de nous, prophétique par les stigmates d'une dévastation dont nous ne percevons encore que les grondements annonciateurs, prophétique aussi par la mise en place d'une génération possible en dehors de toute idéologie de la transgression qui ne fonctionne qu'à l'ombre de la loi. La même démarche à la fois créatrice de désert et d'oasis. Les corps y sont à la fois véhicules et réceptacles. Simultanément ternes et lumineux. Miroirs-mâchoires non pas pour capter en réfléchissant, ce qui est le rôle des miroirs-institutions-médiations-organisations, mais pour fragmenter en libérant à l'infini sans permettre à quelque résidu de se constituer en totalité.

"Conseils Syndicats Gouvernements de la terre. Payez - Rendez la couleur que vous avez prise. Payez Rouge - Rendez le rouge que vous avez volé pour vos drapeaux menteurs et vos enseignes de Coca-Cola - Rendez ce rouge aux pénis et au soleil. Payez Bleu - Rendez le bleu que vous avez volé et stocké le bleu que vous avez parcimonieusement versé dans les compte-gouttes de came - Rendez le bleu que vous avez volé pour vos uniformes de policiers - Rendez ce bleu à la mer et au ciel et aux yeux de la terre. Payez Vert - Rendez le vert que vous avez volé pour votre argent - Rendez ce vert aux fleurs et à la jungle, à la rivière et au ciel. Conseils Syndicats Gouvernements de la terre rendez les couleurs que vous avez volées - Rendez la Couleur.'

En 1888 Van Gogh disait de la peinture : 'Enfin elle promet la couleur''. Aujourd'hui, nous le savons tous, la restitution de la couleur doit passer par la politique. Tour de force impossible? Pourquoi, alors que nos régimes bourgeois en ont réussi un autre, bien plus impensable, celui de faire de la platitude un monument?

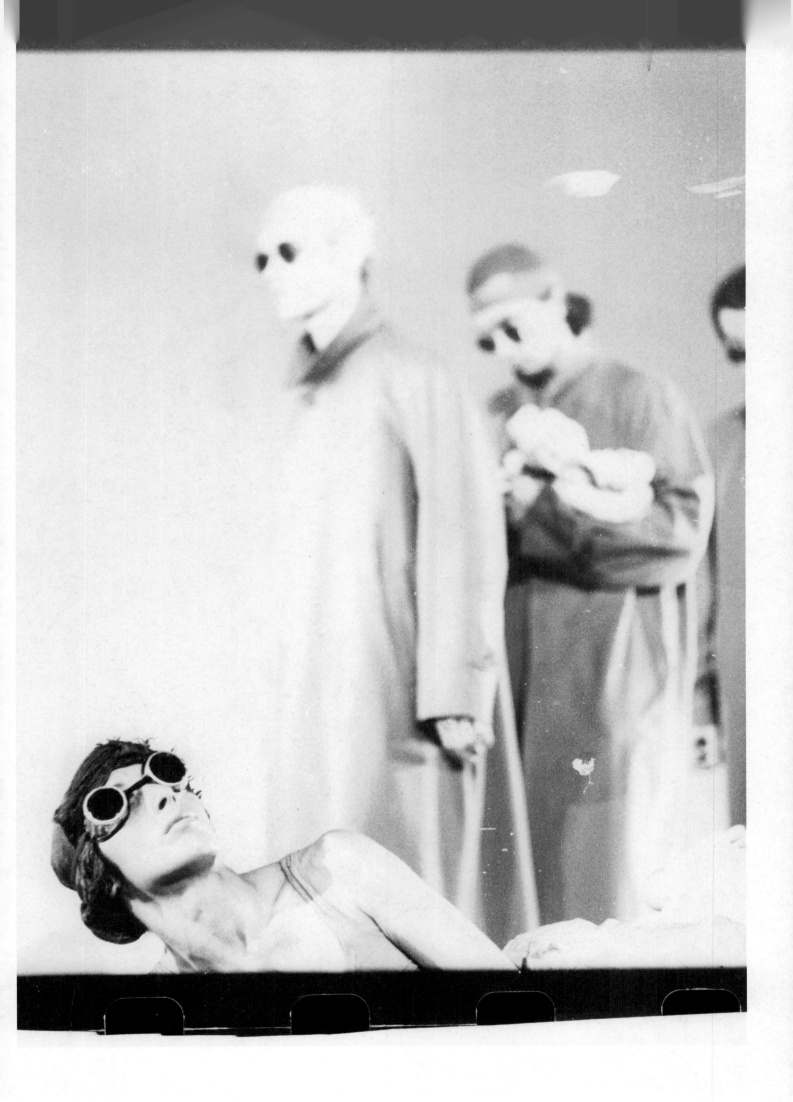

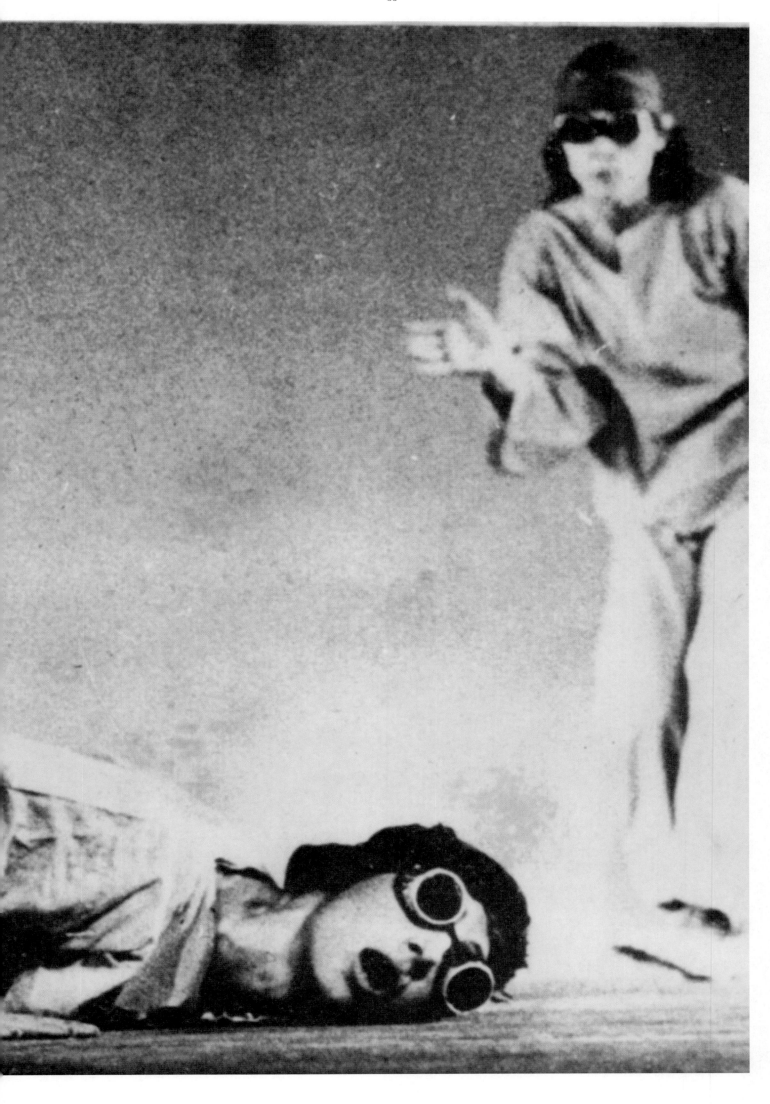

1975:   Poland, training course with the director Jerzy Grotowski
1977:   New York, discovery of Steve Paxton at St Mark's Church
1977:   Creation of *Dispersion*

DISPERSION
Choreography: Pierre Droulers
With: Diane Broman, Juliana Carneiro da Cunha, Pierre Droulers,
Nicole Mossoux, Christophe Requillart, Danielle Cousins
Music: Christian Coppin
Set design and costumes: Groupe Triangles
Lighting: Hubert Dombrecht
First performance: 20 April 1977, Théâtre de Poche, Brussels

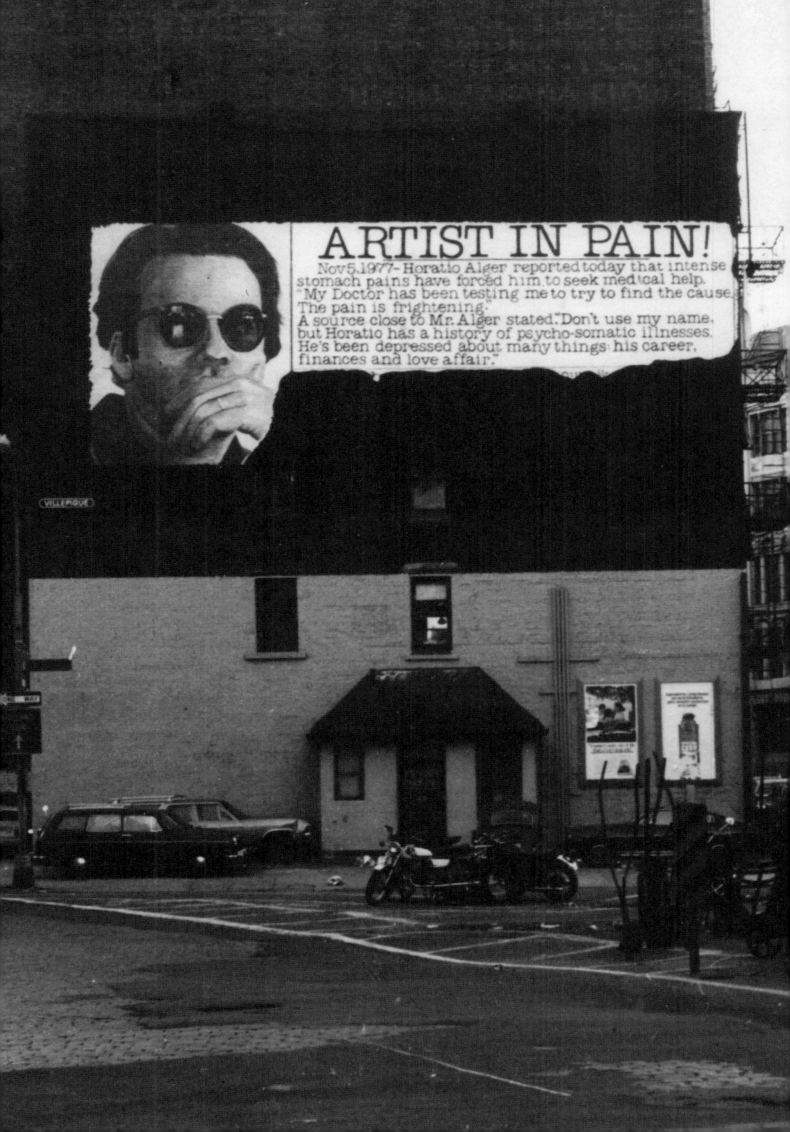

(Bruxelles)

autre chambre à Bruxelles

ART
ENSEMBLE
OF CHICAGO
CERTAIN
BLACKS

"dispersion" 1977

carmelo bene
dramaturgie

DISPERSION
1977

John GIORNO
grasping at emptyness
pp 82–96 in Special
Schizo-Culture issue,
Semiotexte Volume 3
number 2, 1978. Parmi
les contributeurs, William S.
Burroughs, "The limits of control",
John Cage, John Giorno,
Philip Glass, The Ramones,
Robert Wilson.

Arthur & Johnny

Jerzy   Bob
Grotowsky Wilson

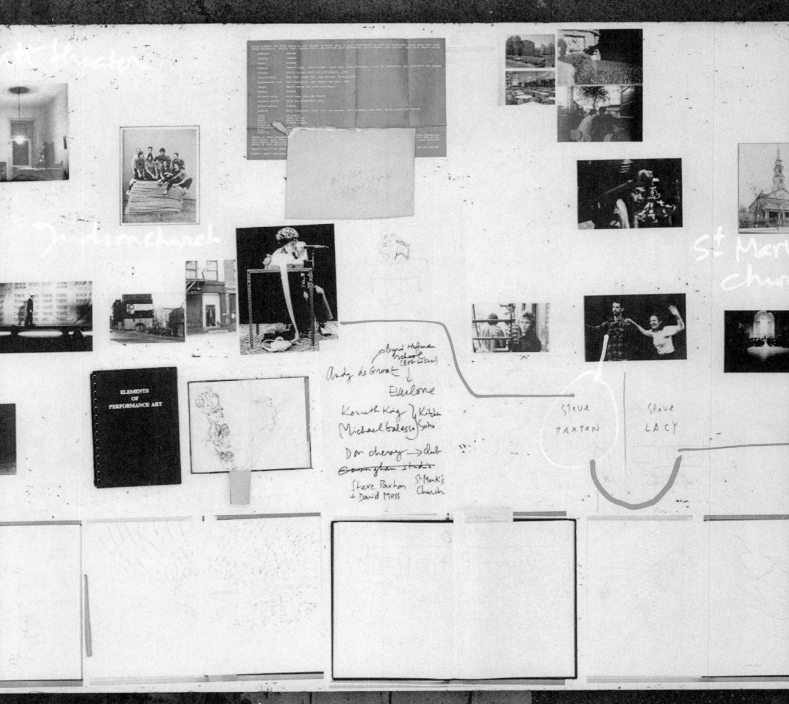

New York

Johnny Rotten

Arthur Rimbaud   One of them embodies the energy of anger, the other inspiration (anger transformed)

RELIGION II, 1978

Stained glass windows keep the cold outside
While the hypocrites hide inside
With the lies of statues in their minds
Where the Christian religion made them blind
Where they hide
And prey to the God of a bitch
spelled backwards is dog
Not for one race, one creed, one world
But for money
Effective
Absurd

Do you pray to the Holy Ghost when you suck your host
Do you read who's dead in the Irish Post
Do you give away the cash you can't afford
On bended knees and pray to lord

Fat pig priest
Sanctimonious smiles
He takes the money
You take the lies

This is religion and Jesus Christ
This is religion cheaply priced
This is bibles full of libel
This is sin in eternal hymn
This is what they've done
This is your religion
The apostles were eleven
Now there's a sod in Heaven

This is religion
There's a liar on the altar
The sermon never falter
This is religion
Your religion

MATIN, UNE SAISON EN ENFER

N'eus-je pas *une fois*
une jeunesse aimable, héroïque,
fabuleuse, à écrire sur des feuilles
d'or, — trop de chance!
Par quel crime, par quelle erreur,
ai-je mérité ma faiblesse actuelle?
Vous qui prétendez que des bêtes
poussent des sanglots de chagrin,
que des malades désespèrent,
que des morts rêvent mal, tâchez
de raconter ma chute et mon sommeil.
Moi, je ne puis pas plus m'expliquer
que le mendiant avec ses continuels
Pater et *Ave Maria*.
Je ne sais plus parler !
Pourtant, aujourd'hui, je crois avoir
fini la relation de mon enfer. C'était
bien l'enfer; l'ancien, celui dont le
fils de l'homme ouvrit les portes.
Du même désert, à la même nuit,
toujours mes yeux las se réveillent
à l'étoile d'argent, toujours, sans
que s'émeuvent les Rois de la vie,
les trois mages, le cœur l'âme,
l'esprit. Quand irons-nous,
par delà les grèves et les monts,
saluer la naissance du travail
nouveau, la sagesse nouvelle,
la fuite des tyrans et des
démons, la fin de la superstition,
adorer — les premiers! —
Noël sur la terre!
Le chant des cieux,
la marche des peuples!
Esclaves, ne maudissons pas la vie.

IF YOU ARE
NAKED
AND SHUT
IN A ROOM.
AND CANNOT
TALK
YOU CAN MAKE
A PIECE WITH
YOUR BODY
AGAINST
THE WALL

Jerzy Grotowski

Robert Wilson

One of them pushes the body to its extremes in order to simplify a performance;
the other slows down the body to create a heightened understanding of space and time

Andy de Groat → Bynd Hoffman school (Bob Wilson)

↓

Everyone

Kenneth King ⎫ Kitchen
(Michael Galasso) ⎬ Soho

Don cherry ——→ club

~~Cunningham studio~~

Steve Paxton + David Moss

St Mark's Church

1979:   Meeting with Steve Lacy in Paris
1979:   Creation of *Hedges*
1980:   Participation in the project *Appartement à louer* by Michel François
1980:   Creation of *Tao*

HEDGES
Choreography: Pierre Droulers
With: Pierre Droulers
Live music: Steve Lacy
Set design: Pierre Droulers, Robert Droulers
Lighting: Hubert Dombrecht
First performance: October 1979, Festival International de Théâtre, Plan K, Brussels

TAO
Choreography: Pierre Droulers
With: Pierre Droulers, Sheryl Sutton
Live music: Steve Lacy
Set design: Brion Gysin
Lighting: Hubert Dombrecht
First performance: 1980, Festival du Marais, Centre Wallonie-Bruxelles, Paris

Bruxelles

HEDGES
1979

« HEDGES »
(DANSES ET PETITES DANSES)

Pierre DROULERS: danses
Steve LACY: saxophone
Hubert DOMBRECHT: éclairage

à la RAFFINERIE DU PLAN K
21, rue de Manchester - 1070 BRUXELLES
Du 10 au 15 juin inclus à 20 h 30

avec l'aide du Ministère de la Communauté Française de Belgique, de la
Commission Française de la Culture de l'Agglomération Bruxelloise, de la
ville de Bruxelles.
Une co-production du groupe TRIANGLES.

STEVE LACY
SEXTET

AU PLAN K
JOY DIVISION
+ DIGITAL DANCE

SILENCE

Bruxelles
Gare du midi

fêtes à Bruxelles

Paris

fêtes à Paris

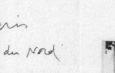

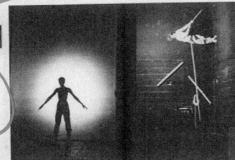

Gare du midi

Gare du Nord

Appartement à louer, Michel François

Ann Veronica Janssens

1981:   Creation of *Tips* with the future Grand Magasin
1982:   Creation of *Pieces for Nothing* with Minimal Compact
1982:   Tour of *Hedges* in Italy and holiday

TIPS
Choreography: Pierre Droulers
With: Pierre Droulers, François Hiffler, Pascale Murtin
Live music: Steve Lacy, Steve Potts
Costumes: Groupe Triangles
First performance: May 1981, Festival d'Évreux

PIECES FOR NOTHING
Choreography: Pierre Droulers
With: Caroline Camus, Pierre Droulers, Didier Silhol
Live music: Minimal Compact
Set design: Philippe Mahillon
Costumes: Anne Frère
Lighting: Jean-Luc Breuer
First performance: 26 May 1982, Festival d'Évreux

Brothers and sisters

marc T.

Gare Mil...

TIPS

Pascale Martin

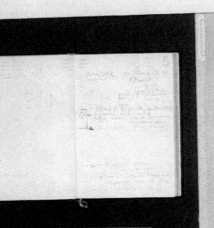

François Hiffler

Steve
Eric

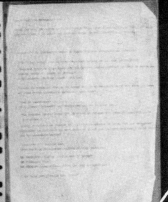

Nathalie W.
Paul. D
Sophie R

PIECE FOR
NOTHING
1982

11 APRIL 2011

A woman sleeps, her face in the soup
David Bowie on avenue Louise
The really hard floor of Woluwe-Saint-Pierre
A ghost and a fall from a moped on Île d'Yeu
Decapitating shrimps in Ostend
Paris-Aix-en-Provence, standing up in the night train
Steve Lacy's telescopic front
A siesta after the Binche Carnival

ARTHUR   RIMBAUD

°ROYAUTÉ° FROM ILLUMINATIONS

Un beau matin, chez un peuple fort doux, un homme et une femme superbes
criaient sur la place publique. °Mes amis, je veux qu'elle soit reine!°
°Je veux être reine!° Elle riait et tremblait. Il parlait aux amis
de révélation, d'épreuve terminée. Ils se pâmaient l'un contre l'autre.

En effet, ils furent rois toute une matinée où les tentures carminées
se relevèrent sur les maisons, et toute l'après-midi, où ils s'avancèrent
du côté des jardins de palmes.

Minimal Compact

1983: Creation of *La Jetée*
1984: Creation of *Miserere*

LA JETÉE
Choreography: Pierre Droulers
With: Patrick Beckers, Pierre Droulers, Michèle Noiret, Eric Sleichim, Sheryl Sutton
Soundtrack: Ricardo Castro
Set design: Jean-Marie Fievez
Costumes: Anne Frère
Lighting: Hubert Dombrecht
First performance: 2 June 1983, Plan K, Brussels
Co-production: Festival de Châteauvallon

MISERERE
Choreography: Pierre Droulers
With: Adriana Borriello, Sussan Deyhim, Pierre Droulers, Kazuya Sato, Winston Tong
Music: Winston Tong, Sussan Deyhim
Dramatic adaptation: Winston Tong (booklet, *Miserere, The Reflections of Orpheus and Eurydice*)
Set design: Paul Gonze
Costumes: Anne Frère
Lighting: Hubert Dombrecht, Xavier Lauwers
First performance: June 1984, Festival du Marais, Centre Wallonie-Bruxelles, Paris
Co-production: Festival de Danse de Châteauvallon

Blues

LA JETÉE
1983

L'Artésienne de Knocke-le-Zoute

mélancolie

MAURICE BEJART

Bruxelles, le 23 décembre 1983

SM/ok

Monsieur le Ministre de la
Culture Ph. MOUREAUX
Cabinet du Ministre,
Avenue des Arts, 19 A/D
1040   BRUXELLES

Monsieur le Ministre,

En tant que Directeur du
Ballet du XXe Siècle, j'aimerais appuyer le travail
de Pierre Droulers, ancien élève de mon école MUDRA
et qui est à la tête actuellement d'une compagnie
de danse.

J'estime que Pierre Droulers
est tout à fait représentatif de la jeune chorégraphie.

Je serais très heureux s'il
pouvait être soutenu de façon plus régulière par les
services de la Culture, section Danse.

En vous remerciant d'avance
de votre aide, je vous prie de croire à l'assurance
de ma meilleure considération.

Maurice Béjart.

20 APRIL 2011

When did Pierre Droulers first push open the door to the office of Bénédicte Pesle, Artservice International, rue du Pré-aux-Clercs?

The door that stuck a bit.

How did he get there?

After his time spent at the Cunningham studio in New York, or after a workshop with Bob Wilson? Or both?

Companion, representative of both artists (and others), Bénédicte Pesle is always the one we want to convince.

Was it at the end of the 1970s?

And Pierre Droulers and Steve Lacy?

Yes, together, a remarkable visible and audible nervous energy spins the air.

Hedges? But when?

With Bénédicte, we went to the Évreux Theatre.

Tips? A Rubik's Cube floats in my memory.

First meeting with Pascale Murtin and François Hiffler, before Grand Magasin.

Sometime later at the Châteauvallon Festival, *La Jetée*, night and mist, Sheryl Sutton.

I remember that I invited Pierre to the Bastille Theatre.

In 1985? It was *Midi-Minuit* with Adriana Borriello. Night, still the night, but already like twilight.

The names of Rilke and Hölderlin come back to me.

I still haven't read them, or not much. Does Pierre Droulers talk to me about them?

Then, for a long time I didn't see his work.

And the light.

The town transformed into pure poetry. Dance defining the space which dances.

The emerging alchemy of a tightrope walker.

Later, at the Cité Internationale, he wove together shadow and light to an incredible degree.

And established dance tuned to an infinite serenity, in a fusion of contradictions: the solid and the immaterial, the physical, concrete exterior and the sensitive, sensorial interior – but also the sensitive, sensorial exterior and the physical, concrete interior – space joined with bodies. One sliding into the other, merging here to re-emerge there, by invisible means, through ethereal shrouds.

No portrayals nor literary references.

No associations nor images.

The intense stripped-back experience of presence, of presences.

Those in the light, and mine.
My body present, bodies engaged in the light and in their time.
From the dark to the light to the dark to the light, everlasting.
To be and not to be. Do and don't do.
Without words.
Free. Freedom fighter.

je commence à collectionner
c'est un signe de vieillesse

quand j'imagine le futur.
je vois rien
ou plutôt le noir.
je nepeux que travailler
c'est mon garde-fou

Steve, mon maître

the distance between two stars
la distance qui sépare deux étoiles
might be the distillation of emotion
serait une distillation de l'émotion
and chagrin the rush of flame
et le chagrin un jet de flamme
between a comet and a nova
unissant comète à nova

Miserere poems, Winston Tong

Kazuya Sato

KAZUYA   SATO

18 FEBRUARY 2011

ありがと

LOVE to YOU

1985:   Creation of *Midi-Minuit*
1986:   Travel in Japan
1986:   Act in *Face-à-Face* by Michèle Anne De Mey
1988:   Choreography for video clip for Lio's *Les brunes comptent pas pour des prunes*
1988:   Travel in India
1989:   Creation of *Miettes et Mouettes*
1989:   Act in *Ottone Ottone* by Anne Teresa De Keersmaeker

MIDI-MINUIT
Choreography: Pierre Droulers
With: Adriana Borriello, Pierre Droulers
Music: Sussan Deyhim, Ghédalia Tazartès
Costumes: Anne Frère, Paul Droulers
Lighting: Gérard Poli
First performance: 16 April 1985, Théâtre de la Bastille, Paris

MIETTES ET MOUETTES
Set design and choreography: Pierre Droulers, Charlie Degotte
With: Charlie Degotte
First performance: 1989, Théâtre de la Balsamine, Brussels

ARTSERVICE INTERNATIONAL

ASSOCIATION RÉGIE PAR LA LOI DE 1901

16, RUE DU PRÉ-AUX-CLERCS, 75007 PARIS - TÉL. (1) 544.17.09

TELEX : PUBLI BTI PARIS 250.302 COMPTE 11/18.9269 ARTSINT

M. Pierre DROULERS
29, rue du College
B - 1050 BRUXELLES

Paris, le 21 septembre 1984

Cher Pierre,

Dès réception de votre lettre j'ai appelé Denis Seigneur, le responsable des bourses "Villa Medecis hors les murs".

Il est très possible que vous receviez une bourse de voyage pour le Japon et même la Chine si vous savez comment on peut rentrer en Chine.

Il faudrait qu'immédiatement vous envoyez à Denis Seigneur, 34 rue de la Pérouse, 75016 Paris, une notice biographique et documentation brève sur votre travail passé (j'ai mentionné que vous sortiez de Mudra ce qui a fait très bon effet) mais surtout une note d'intention sur ce voyage, durée (qui peut être de 3, 6 ou 9 mois) et personnes au Japon qui pourraient vous accueillir et assurer que votre séjour sera efficace.

Il faut faire vite car les décisions doivent être prises avant la fin de l'année et naturellement, il y a d'autres candidats.

Bien amicalement,

Bénédicte PESLE

26 dec. 1988

Ce soir
l'ampoule de la
lampe de poche Mazda
a brûlé

Si on avait su
on aurait pris une
Wonder

1989:   Record with Michael Lonsdale, *Digue* by Christian Dotremont
1991:   Creation of *Remains*

REMAINS
Choreography: Pierre Droulers
With: Pierre Droulers
Live music: Steve Lacy
Set design: Pierre Droulers
Assistant: Toula Limnaios
Lighting: Pierre Droulers
First performance: 5 April 1991, Musée de Toulon, Toulon, Festival de Châteauvallon
Co-production: Les Brigittines, as part of Bruxelles Centra(a)l

A
M. LONSDALE - DIGUE

N.R □ ☒ ES

MX 90
POSITION·METAL
JAPAN·JAPON

maxell

les fantômes mécaniques.

le + grand
comédien du monde

CHRISTIAN DOTREMONT

D I G U E

AVEC DES PHOTOGRAPHIES D'
OSCAR SCHELLEKENS

1959

" JE SUIS CELUI QUI TOUJOURS VEUT PARTIR

ET QUI RESTE, RESTE, RESTE. "

Adaptation libre du poéme de FERNANDO PESSOA :

" Le passage des heures " in Les Poésies d'ALVARO de CAMPOS.

Réalisatrice:

Cécile PATINGRE

48 rue Sedaine

750II PARIS

tel: 48 06 40 45

Chorégraphe:

Pierre DROULERS

IO4 rue du Chemin- Vert

750II PARIS

tel: 43 55 27 93

1

JAMES ENSOR
"Mon portrait en 1960", 1880

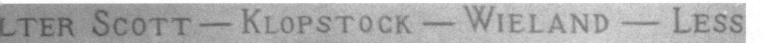

Je soussigné Pierre Dronlen avoir reçu la somme de 1 341 650 Lires pour les représentations de "Remains" les 4 et 5 août à Castiglioncello.

JMoulers.

Je soussigné Frédérique Laguy avoir reçu la somme de 627 100 Lires pour les représentations de "Remains" à _____ les 4 et 5 août 1991.

6 août 91

Je soussigné Steve Lacy avoir reçu la somme de 1 821 210 £ soit 41 000 F.B. pour les représentations de "Remains" à Castiglioncello.

Steve Lacy

1991:   Creation of *Comme si on était leurs petits poucets*
1992:   Creation of *Humeurs*
1993:   Creation of *Jamais de l'abîme*

COMME SI ON ÉTAIT LEURS PETITS POUCETS
Choreography and set design: Pierre Droulers
With: Amy Garmon, Roberto Graiff, Anne Huwaert, Monica Marti, Fernando Martin, Simonne Moesen (assistant)
Direction: Toula Limnaios
Artistic direction, assistant: Alain Rigout
Music: Pierre Droulers, selected from 78 rpm records
Set design: Pierre Droulers, Pierrot Tkao
Collaboration: Nadine Ganase, Toula Limnaios
Costumes: Anne Frère
Lighting: Xavier Lauwers, Philippe Baste
First performance: 11 September 1991, Festival La Bâtie, Geneva
Co-production: Charleroi/Danses, Festival La Bâtie - Genève, Festival d'Octobre en Normandie, Indigo

HUMEURS
Choreography: Pierre Droulers
With: Pierre Droulers, Anne Huwaert (taken up by Stefan Dreher, Celia Hope Simpson)
Music: Captain Tobias Hume
First performance: 1992, Théâtre National de Bretagne, Rennes

JAMAIS DE L'ABÎME
Choreography: Pierre Droulers
With: Amy Garmon, Liv Hanne Haugen, Anne Huwaert, Simonne Moesen, Guillaume Rannou, Jean-Christophe Térol, Franz Weger
Direction, assistant: Leslie Maerschalok
Music: Baudouin de Jaer
Music, assistants: Alain Rigout, Hélène Sage
Set design: Pierre Droulers, Pierrot Tkao
Costumes: Anne Frère, assisted by Delia Fleischuer
Lighting: Xavier Lauwers, Pascale Burlet
First performance: 28 January 1993, Palais des Beaux-Arts, Charleroi
Co-production: Charleroi/Danses, Biennale Nationale de Danse du Val-de-Marne,
Centre Culturel d'Orly Aragon-Triolet, Théâtre d'Évreux-Scène Nationale

alain Rigout

COMME SI ON
ETAIT LEURS
PETITS
POUCETS
1991

again

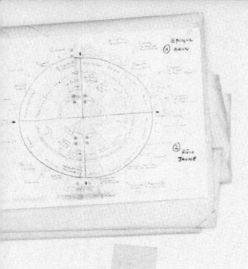

DE
ME
993

HUMEUR
1995

DU MONDE ENTIER

JAMES JOYCE

FINNEGANS
WAKE

ROMAN
TRADUIT DE L'ANGLAIS
ET PRÉSENTÉ
PAR PHILIPPE LAVERGNE

nrf

GALLIMARD

Alain Rigout

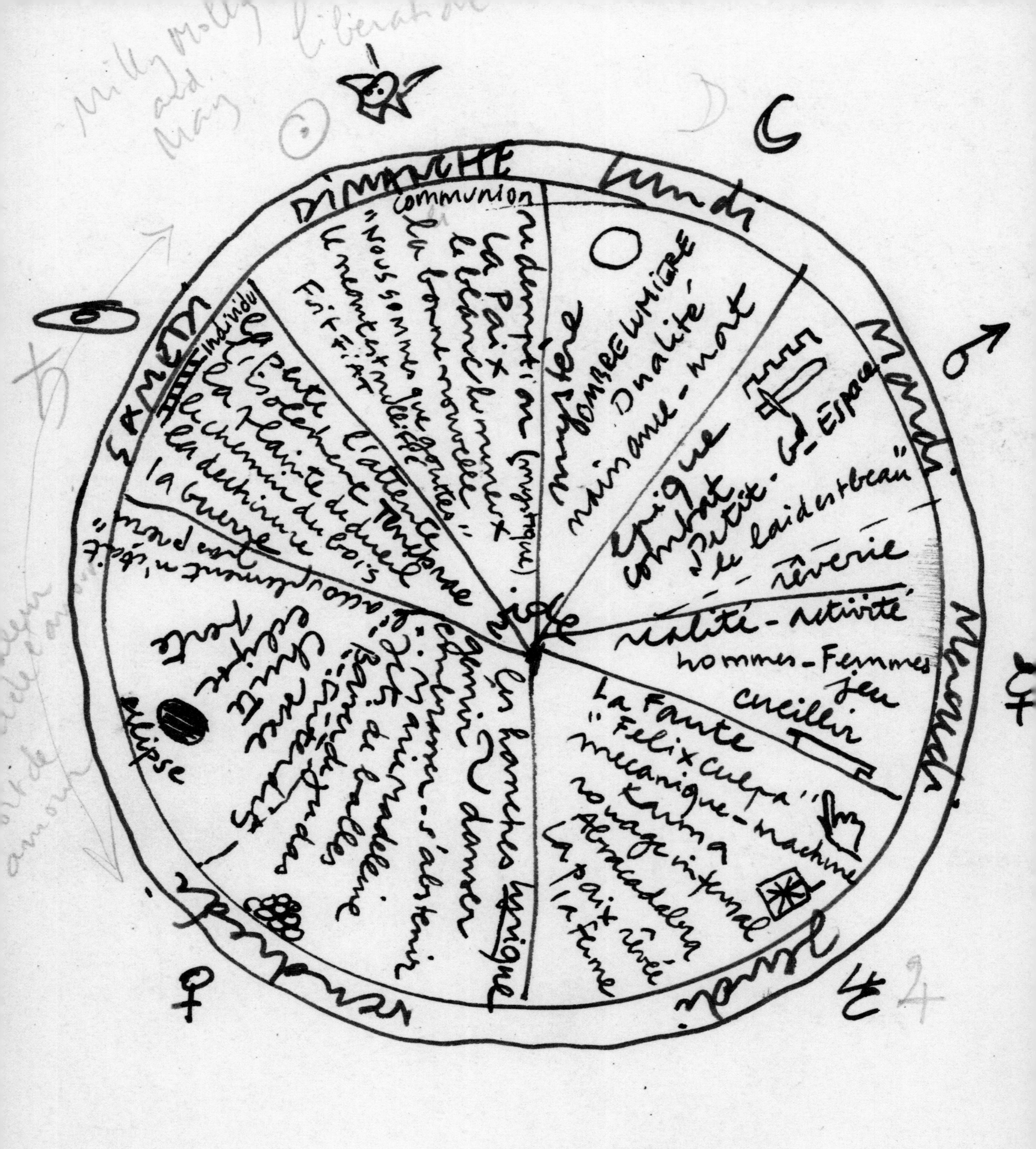

lune = reflexion rythme
Mars = activité, energie
Mercure = communication
Jupiter = expansion
Venus = feeling
Saturne = formation
Sun = totalité, dieu

BUFFON

le laid est beau

dimanche · lundi · mardi · jeudi · vendredi · samedi

mystère
ombre – lumière
dualité
maître – mourir
logique
combat
espace
grandeur – ciel

LA CHUTE

"Bababadalgharaghtakamminarronnkonntonerroontuonthunntrovarrhovnawnskawntoohoordenenthurnuk"

Cette chute participe du premier chant finnois du Kalevala. Lasse de sa solitude, la Fille de l'Air s'était endormie dans les eaux maternelles; voyant son genou qui émergeait, une sarcelle y bâtit son nid et pond six oeufs d'or et un septième de fer. Lorsque la jeune fille se réveille, les oeufs roulent et se brisent mais les fragments forment la terre, le ciel, le soleil, la lune et les nuages.

Les cent lettres qui composent ce premier tonnerre sont l'écho de cette création.

James Joyce

CHAPTER TWO

MATERIAL DREAMS

CONVERSATION

MICHEL FRANÇOIS: Everything began with an extraordinary project (he laughs) which was called *Appartement à louer*. It was put on at the boulevard de Régent in 1979. It involved transforming an exhibition space into an apartment. The apartment had to be open for visitors day and night and we needed a couple to live there. The space being virtually unusable, I talked to the actors and dancers. Artists had put together the design, each of them looking after one room (bedroom, kitchen, bathroom, hallway). The appearance of the interior objects, of the furniture, was highlighted, beyond their actual function.

The fictional couple who were living in the apartment had to receive visitors. They could be watched or disturbed in the night during their sleep. It was extremely difficult. After a few days, the actor, Patrick Beckers, was exhausted. We then put together teams that lasted a week at a time. That was how Pierre Droulers came on the scene. Me, I was also there to manage things, open the door, etc.

ANN VERONICA JANSSENS: I didn't directly take part in the project but I helped out as a friend, an audience member, as well as occasionally a supplier of food. The space was organised by the artists in a non-functional manner. In the sitting room, for example, the whole space was designed to point towards the television screen. The actor's performance in such an urban context (on display), homely and absurd, was an experience of fun, of space and of movement, very experimental, strong, radical.

PIERRE DROULERS: It was amusing for us because it was supposed to be our own environment. We explained to the visitors that we liked that, us, this artificial space, the malfunctioning television… We said it was great! The visitors were puzzled… (he laughs)

AVJ: It was a performance that lasted three weeks, up until the actors and all the participants were exhausted.

MF: The model used was the representations of living spaces that we see today in furniture showrooms or superstores. They construct living spaces and we think we are in a kitchen or a bedroom. But in fact, it's two-dimensional. As soon as you move a bit you see behind the scenes. It's scenery. This idea of scenery interested me. I began by making studies in the theatre, which I stopped because the theatre itself doesn't interest me very much. What interested me was the staging, the scenery.

This first project was therefore a way of seeing if we could live in a staged setting. And a way of contradicting the natural reflexes of theatrical codes because we can't act for twenty-four hours in a row. It was about pushing these limits. Same thing for the scenery! We needed to be able to eat, put things in the fridge, use the toilets… There was a tension between that which should be functional and that which fell into the artistic domain.

PD: I wonder what led us to meet up again after *Appartement à louer*.

FABIENNE AUCANT: The following collaboration took place sixteen years later, in 1995, with *Mountain/Fountain*. In the meantime, you often met up, notably in Michel and Ann Veronica's house and studio, rue Joseph Bens in Brussels. For Pierre, it was a mythical place.

PD: Yes. 'Bens' is an artist's studio, connected to the house, looking out over a garden, and open to everyone. I came with friends, and I found myself as a young artist side by side with other artists who opened up their studios. I think that I arrived at Bens without really thinking, a bit like when my father took me as a child to Eugène Leroy's or Eugène Dodeigne's house on a Sunday morning in the north of France. And then, it was there that I began to see your work. I was told afterwards that the French gallery owners, or the artists that followed you, loved coming to Brussels, because there one could go straight into the kitchens or into the gardens of artists. In Paris, it's more stilted, you need to make an appointment, we see each other in offices or galleries. At Bens, there was this conviviality, this exultation in a shared vision.
Making my way, I had the impression to have known you through a situation that allowed me to understand your work, before we actually worked together. I also discovered the couple Michel François/Ann Veronica Janssens, two very different artists but who worked collectively. Deep down, I said to myself: it's the perfect couple! On one side it's action, making things, and on the other it's contemplation, stimulating things that are already there (you just had to open a door or knock down a wall). The economics of using little and the economics of action, of objects. This tandem is always a motor for my work! The need to activate, to do things and, at the same time, the necessity in moments of letting go, to look at things in a way that they could be unveiled, removed…

MF: They say that life is rather simple! There is the earth and the sky. We shared that, the high and the low. Me, it was the low (he laughs).

FA: So what triggered the collaboration in 1995?

AVJ: I think it was the *Conte de Mikkaddo* that inspired Pierre.

PD: Yes. I had accumulated an enormous number of objects with my previous piece *Comme si on était leurs petits poucets*, based on a work by James Joyce: mattresses, bikes, wooden beams, bits of wood, a pile of stuff… I fell under the spell of this tale set out that you must tidy up the objects, and group them, naming things, then arranging by solid and hollow to make space. This idea of making space, by eliminating objects, came at just the right time. It was the first piece where I cleared out the theatrical and literary questions. The laboratory was the objects. The tale was used like a handbook, a functional guide. At this period, I was also reading a lot of Francis Ponge.

FA: In what context was this tale written?

MF: That of an exhibition, with a small catalogue published by Marie-Puck Broodthaers. Rather than giving the task of writing a text to someone else, I did it myself. Writing, for me, is a way of understanding what I do from another point of view. It's like giving a title to something that we've made, but longer. The title can come very late on. As a sculptor, we assign a presence to an object, to replace a certain absence. The body of the sculptor is absent. The object is a witness. It's the piece of evidence that demonstrates the initial contact with the material.

PD: One of the first experiments that we conducted with Michel on *Mountain/Fountain* was a workshop in order to break the objects! Michel didn't find it normal that we were always making elegant movements. One time he said, 'We'll set up a little workshop', and he brought along a number of objects to break. So that we could find again a sort of brutality or functionality, with a much more direct movement. From my side, I found that the dance we had was a bit too prepared. There, we restructured ourselves through the work of sculpture and functionality, at the opposite ends of what we had learned.

FA: Pierre, was it about working together with artists in order to dismantle certain foundations of choreography?

PD: Not dismantle. Previously, I had been struck by Bob Wilson's pieces, his work with autists, particularly with Christopher Knowles. In Paris, in the 1970s, I joined his research group Laila. We undertook physical experiments based on repetition, the loss of control. My elder brother also worked with autists. I was impressed by these natural bodies, much more than by completely aestheticised bodies. At heart, I always liked this direct physicality, raw. And paradoxically sophisticated in its incongruity.

FA: How did your collaboration work? Pierre always says that he never gave you a 'commission' and that you weren't a stage designer.

PD: Ann Veronica is not a stage designer. Michel, it's different. He has this affinity with stage design. He likes strategies and make-believe, to make things appear. For example, in *Mountain/Fountain* he had the idea of a sloping stage. Whereas Ann Veronica suspended the project for *De l'air et du vent*, saying to me: 'I am not a stage designer, I am an artist.' She didn't want to start to organise the stage, the backdrop, find ways of using the mirrors, etc.

MF: We were in Brazil during the preperations for *Mountain/Fountain*. I didn't think that I was hired as the stage designer. I thought that Pierre wanted to start a conversation with me and to exchange ideas, like a game of table tennis. I never thought about the stage except for the performance. I rather put down on paper some actions, some statements or mini-performances. I remember having sent 150 proposals. Pierre is right to say that I was sometimes irritated by the dancers' gestures: for example, we had a large sack of confetti and I proposed that a dancer throw the confetti in his face. Straight away, the dancer's gesture was elegant and not very vigorous. I said to him: 'No, why can't you throw confetti in your face normally?' (he laughs)

PD: So Michel did it! We were all astounded. He threw confetti in his face like pecking pigeons.

MF: There was something else that shocked me a bit in this first collaboration with a choreographer - it was seeing that the dancers didn't smile at all. When a dancer arrives at the edge of the stage, it all seems serious, he is so absorbed… I asked myself if there wasn't a way of being more natural, to have a certain complicity with the audience. I frankly really like the idea that an actor can be there. Take account that we are there, here and now, and not to make an abstraction of the audience. To think of theatre as a shared moment of life, without a curtain or traditions that keep us apart.

AVJ: Pierre came to find me before the composition of *De l'air et du vent*. For my part, it was a first experience with a choreographer. He spoke to me about the texts and films that had inspired him. I had no experience of the stage. For me it wasn't about constructing a set. The concerns for my work were the experiences of space, of the light that filtered within the architectural material, the possibilities of making the material seem more fluid. That became more actual during the first week of collaboration in a theatre, where I arrived with materials and experiments. Pierre worked with the dancers. I had a problem with the angles, the two-dimensional staging relationship and the front of the stage that separated the stage from the public. I had the feeling that I wouldn't be able to propose a solution that was compatible with the choreography. I made some suggestions but, when the dancers entered the stage, it didn't work. The required experience was disrupted. From that point we discussed it together and then we carried on, adopting some working methods that interested Pierre, in order to encourage and relaunch our collaboration on a new footing.

PD: There was an image. I had stopped on the motorway between Paris and Brussels. I had photographed a field that was covered with a plastic sheet. It reflected the sky. The horizon disappeared. The sky and the earth were united. From that photo, Ann Veronica worked on the make-up of the floor and backdrop in a way to build a stage that had no sharp angles. This image had provided a living space for *De l'air et du vent*.

AVJ: Yes, in which the light was diffused, became iridescent. After this initial experience, Pierre used me again for the project *MA* and *MA-I*. He understood my difficulties very well. He explained the project MA to me, the idea of the threshold, of time lapse. In the context of the complete freedom that he had in Tours, he asked me to produce an installation called *MA-I*. It was then that I produced my first coloured fog.

F.A: Is that to say that this collaboration with Pierre introduced colour?

AVJ: (silence) I was lucky because there was a terrific creative lighting engineer in the team, Jim Clayburgh, and a stage space at my disposal. Within the idea of the Japanese concept of *MA*, that's to say threshold, Jim had helped with the fine-tuning of the light and colour variations. The spectators entered from the backstage area, on to the stage, where they were plunged into a coloured fog that created another conception of space, of sense, of the length of time, of movement. I had suggested, as a basis for the colour, coloured variations of a sunset at a forty-five-degree angle, taken from an aerial photograph. We walked on into an orangey-yellow, amber, and the colours then dissolved into a dark violet-blue.

PD: The audience entered from the back of the theatre, the auditorium was empty. They were immediately plunged into the fog. They were experimenting with virtual choreography.

AVJ: The audience was trying to become familiar with unknown territory. They were the dancers!

MF: As a choreographer, it must have been pleasing to see that spectators could become dancers. The fact of being in the fog, feeling your way forward, and then bumping into someone at the last moment.

PD: Yes, and also there were noises, the sound of voices. For *MA*, I had this ideal image of fog. But we couldn't reproduce it in a classical Italian-style theatre. Ann Veronica's installation *MA-I* allowed us to create this image. In the relationship between warm light/cold light, there was this moment that I found magnificent, the transition from yellow to blue. There was a complete greyness, which was the fog itself, which swung between cold and warm. It was a rather radical experience. We had completely subverted choreographic performance.

FA: What brought you together in this collaboration, and even beyond that, was the work with perception, the feeling of the body and of presence. Another subversion or another interconnection in this relationship between the dance stage, the studio and the installation space, was also Michel's idea in *MA* to reproduce your rehearsal studio onstage.

P.D: Yes, we built an identical version on stage, keeping the correct proportions, the doors, of our studio in the rue des Ateliers in Brussels. Suddenly, our rehearsal and work space was the stage itself, the staging of *MA* one and the same thing. We remained in our workshop when we were on tour. We didn't have to readjust to a different space.

FA: *MA* involved a creative process that lasted nine months. Ann Veronica and Michel followed the process. You weren't there every day, but went to watch rehearsals frequently. There was an organic link, a sort of mentoring.

MF: It was Pierre's nature and wish that meant that it happened like that. He always more or less involved us, sometimes in a more distant way. We were always invited to attend a rehearsal or a discussion. With great loyalty. I must say that, compared to filmmakers or directors, it's the choreographers who call most often on artists to collaborate on their projects.

   The question of time is very different for artists and for dramatic artists. With art, there is a sort of immediateness. You remain a quarter of a second in front of a picture or you stay for hours, but in the end it's the spectator who manages his time.

AVJ: … whereas in the theatre or with dance, there is a form of chronology, of storytelling, an act of writing, a written length of time.

PD: We work with time length. We calculate the length of time. We work with this length of time so that the spectator can feel involved in an idea.

MF: That assumes absolutely different conventions.

PD: In *MA* I very much liked the images you made of cars. Each car, at a certain moment, flashed a reflection.

AVJ: Yes, I filmed from a bridge above a motorway, the cars reflecting the rays of a setting sun. It was a very simple take which took a few minutes but, at the same time, there is in the video a very strong image, a sort of spectacular cinematic effect produced by the natural activity of the sun.

PD: In projecting this video in *MA*, there was no question of having any other action on stage at the same time. So, in the performance, suddenly, we close the doors and there is total darkness. We give some time so that the spectator can stop and absorb themselves in this image. We create a sort of isolation bubble. And then we carry on.

FA: Let's talk also about your collaboration in *Suspension temporelle*. This time it was Ann Veronica who invited Pierre to take part in her exhibition at MAC in Marseille in 2003.

AVJ: I found that it made sense that we continued to cross-pollinate our two disciplines. I had a solo exhibition called *8'26''* in Marseille. I felt

it was important to investigate the body in action, that of the visitor and also that of the creator. With Pierre, this question presented itself in a very concrete way. He made a proposal specifically for the evening, as the museum was closing, and which then repeated itself for the whole length of the exhibition.

MF: Not something that was done very often at the time.

PD: What I wanted to do, was at the moment when the visitors were leaving the exhibition, at the moment the doors were closing, there was a pause and that people could not leave straight away. That there would be a confinement, as if they should still have the impression of the experience instilled in them before leaving.

FA: In the spirit of Ann Veronica, you proposed a threshold. Which resounded when activated.

MF: Pierre also has a very baroque side. Profuse, very coloured, fantastical.

PD: That made me think of the Belgian pictorial tradition. It was thanks to Michel and Ann Veronica that I opened up to this artistic tradition. Regularly, Michel spoke to me about Hieronymus Bosch, René Magritte, Marcel Broodthaers. You said that there was a typical lineage from here.

MF: Yes, it's my little theory. The Belgians are caught between two languages: speaking neither totally French nor Dutch, particularly in Brussels which is a bilingual city. It doesn't therefore astonish me that, under circumstances where the language is unstable, or not very reliable, we resort to imagery to accompany speech. For example, why are graphic novels flourishing in Belgium, why is surrealism here so specific and enduring? Words are not enough, we can't completely trust them. We need to add an image to them. Or contextualise the image. At the end of the day, that could also introduce a supplementary instability.

PD: That makes me think again of your Bens house and studio, of the relationship between art and life. Like taking your children on your journeys, exposing them to your experiences. Or Broodthaers who included all the day-to-day data in his work.

FA: That also speaks to you because you come from the north of France and that your father took you around everywhere.

PD: Yes, my father took me to Eugène Leroy's house, he's the artist equivalent of Rabelais. But strangely, that also reminds me of the Americans that we saw arriving in the 1980s. With Robert Rauschenberg, Merce Cunningham… They offered forms of collage, of abstraction, with a literature emptied of all meaning. Bob Wilson is a surrealist who removed all questions of literature in order to capture the physical weaknesses: schizophrenia, lacerations, cries, fog on stage.

In his piece *Overture*, the curtain rises and we see a thick fog of incredible density, uprooted trees, two women start shouting. The space is torn apart. We are in a surrealist vision. But the whole French-leaning literary side was removed. Belgian and French surrealists didn't get on well. For that matter, I am also open to things more pared-down, more zen.

FA: The fact that Pierre's father was a painter has no doubt influenced his tendency to respect the work of artists, to promote them, to know how to use them.

AVJ: Yes, absolutely. He thinks like an artist.

JEAN-MARC ADOLPHE: What does that mean, 'think like an artist'?

MF: We also say 'stupid like an artist'! (he laughs)

AVJ: In any case, Pierre has this interest, this observation of other disciplines. He uses them. He understands them.

MF: He trusts them. He trusts something for its tangibility. It's not only true for his performances. It's also because of his regular visits to studios and exhibitions. There is an exchange. His viewpoint interests me when he comes into the studio.

PD: When we arrive in a studio, we feel directly what's going on, what is preoccupying the artist. Watching my father paint, I also saw very clearly that he was working with time. He rightly said: 'At a certain moment you must stop.' If you don't stop, you make another brushstroke and your painting goes off in another direction. This time period for finishing a work corresponds to a more solitary management between artist and object.

FA: To come back to the question or the phrase 'think like an artist', Hans Theys said that Pierre painted in three dimensions.

PD: Sometimes, the dancers are like paintbrushes in space which draw lines and movement.

JMA: In a certain way, isn't painting itself already in 3D? There is depth…

MF to PD: Have you ever painted?

PD: No, my father was a painter, so I said I would be a dancer. (he laughs)

JMA: Historically, it seems to me that the visual arts felt a certain suspicion in relation to theatre, to dance…

MF and AVJ are not sure.

AVJ: I don't think so. For over a century, there are examples of a cross-over between disciplines.

MF: Yes. But it's true that there is something pejorative when we say, 'Such and such project was too spectacular or too theatrical…'

JMA: The notion of presence is a bit suspect. Often, in the work of visual artists, presence comes through a work. There is a suspicion in relation to an implicit presence.

AVJ: Not necessarily. In my work, the artwork asks questions of the body, the senses, it sends you into an interior space.

JMA: It seems to me that, in Michel's work, the gesture is very important. With Ann's it's maybe more cerebral than physical.

MF: It's true. They are very simple gestures. There are very few objects. Often things that I haven't made myself. The execution maybe delegated. Afterwards, the gesture comes at the moment when the object is about to be put on show, experimented with in space, then shared. Often when my work is brought up, I am told: 'It's the hand, it's the hand.'
But I am not so sure. For example, before coming here, I put a drip containing vinegar above a black marble cube. The acid dissolves the marble, slowly but surely, and it inexorably hollows out the marble. It's a sort of procedure that will last for years. What is the relationship with a gesture or

the hand here? It works without me. It's a form of 'productive inactivity'.
PD: There is an apparatus. Michel makes his drop fall. It's almost as if he
was in the process of putting it there. Often, in your work, Ann Veronica,
I sense more the question of bathing. Going into a space. Not to be led to a
place. Bathing in light, in fog, an opening out.

JMA: With the Japanese emperor in *Conte de Mikkaddo*, then with the title
of *MA*, which is a Japanese concept, we could say that there is something
fundamentally eastern in your respective approaches. A form of presence
that indicates an absence, which is not there to fill space, to fill it up.
But which gives it a density.

FA: In Michel's work, there is this struggle, a dialectic between hollow and
solid.

AVJ: Yes, it's yin and yang. It's not one plus two, but it's a whole, in fact.

PD: When Stefan Dreher performed *Zoo Walking with Rider*, his body is really
a sculpture that doesn't stop twisting and turning, working in a way that
is both complete and hollow. The space in which he performs his dance will
also change the perception that we have. There is the question of outward
space, and interior space, and the relationship between one and the other.
We rediscover this subject with *MA*, when I ask the dancers to define the
space, rather than just make movements.

MF: Something that links us from this point of view is a sort of
incompleteness, the feeling of not being finished.

FA: How would you describe your place within the work and performance of
Pierre Droulers? Ann Veronica, you often speak of infiltration. And you,
Michel, of contamination.

AVJ: I think everything comes from Pierre. It's this relationship that
Pierre has with the arts, his responsiveness that has allowed meetings to
suddenly take place. It's linked to his ability to listen, to pay attention.
A resonance. It was the collaboration with Pierre that opened up choreography
and live art for me. A relationship that I had never established before and
which is part of my work today. I had complete freedom with him. To be able
to propose sometimes difficult and radical forms for a choreographic project.
When the projects stopped, there were still reverberations. Things carried on

PD: Yes, I like the word 'resonance'.

MF: Pierre worked through sedimentation. Things took a long time to filter and to settle. Things re-emerged ten years later. This sort of speed was complicated for me. I talked about *Mountain/Fountain*, which I wrote feverishly in sketches. I had no response from Pierre. There isn't an immediate response, never. He needs to let things marinate. He's not extraordinarily busy. It's a completely different method. If it worked, that's because I accepted that 'he would sleep on it'.

FA: Pierre, you also said that Michel physically helps you to get things going.

PD: I like calling Michel, to be shaken up, to be challenged. Ann Veronica, you, you always lead me back to dance.

AVJ: Yes, I push you into the dance, and you, you always try to impede this movement, to bring back space and plasticity.

PD: That's why I do a lot of meditation! Too many thoughts slow me down. I meditate to be more present.

AVJ: It's also because Pierre is a sculptor. He needs to experiment with all sorts of material, not just the body.

Conversation between Ann Veronica Janssens, Michel François and Pierre Droulers

Interviewed by Fabienne Aucant, with the participation of Jean-Marc Adolphe

La Raffinerie, Brussels, 25 June 2016

1995:   Creation of *Mountain/Fountain*

MOUNTAIN/FOUNTAIN
Choreography: Pierre Droulers
With: Aurélien Desclozeaux, Stefan Dreher, Celia Hope Simpson, Barbara Manzetti, Harry Theaker, Pierre Droulers
Video: Michel François
Music: Baudouin de Jaer, Fabian Fiorini, Thierry De Mey
Set design: Pierre Droulers, Michel François, Christine Grégoire, Thibault Vancraenenbroeck
Set design, assistant: Xavier Leton
Artistic collaboration: Michel François
Costumes: Sabine Kumeling
Lighting: Xavier Lauwers
First performance: 24 March 1995, Palais des Beaux-Arts, Marathon de la danse, Charleroi
Co-production: Charleroi/Danses

MOUNTAIN/
FOUNTAIN
1995

MICHEL
FRANÇOIS

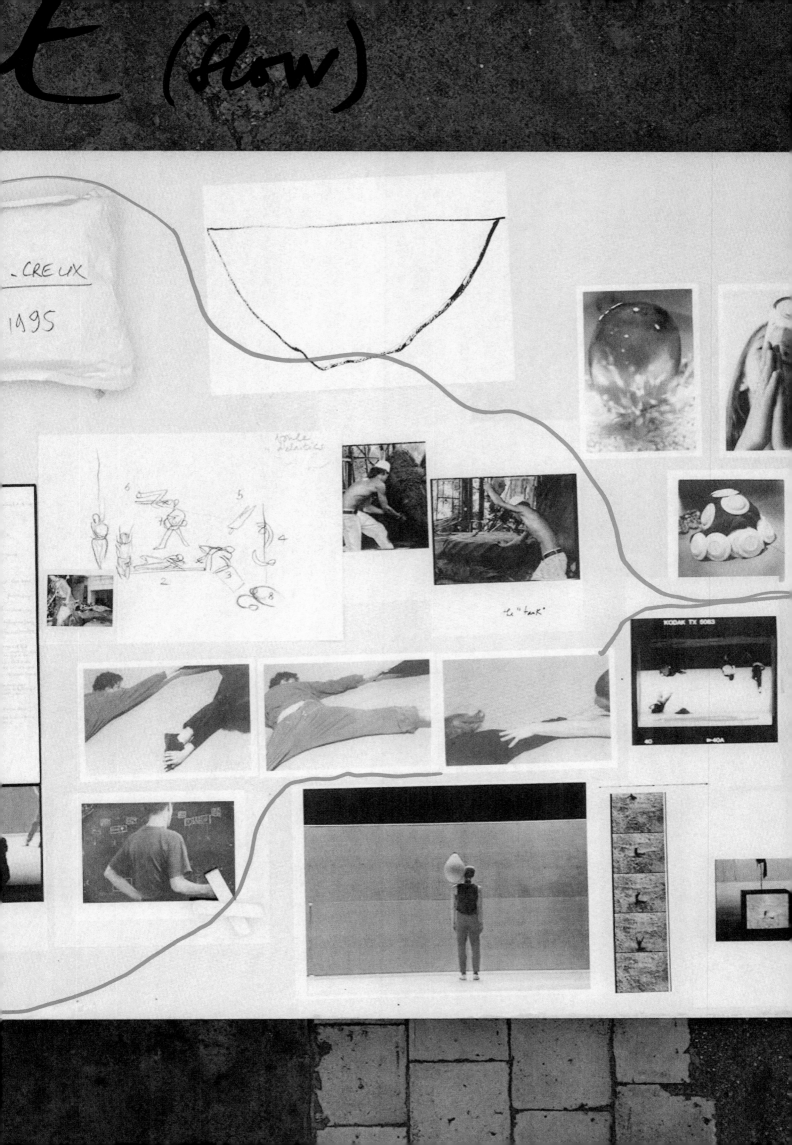

Mikkaddo, empereur du Japon, signa l'unique décret de tout son règne: ordre était donné à tous les membres de son administration de procéder au Grand Inventaire. Il s'agissait pour toute personne de rassembler à proximité du palais chaque chose qu'elle possédait ou qu'elle rencontrait à la surface de l'île.

Ce projet unique avait longuement été mûri par Mikkaddo alors que la perspective du pouvoir se rapprochait. Chacun ignorait ce qui avait motivé un tel plan, mais se gardait bien d'en discuter la sagesse.

Toutes les maisons furent ainsi vidées, afin que leur contenu soit acheminé vers le palais pour y être recensé. Chaque objet était alors isolé momentanément, pour que l'on puisse déterminer collégialement la catégorie à laquelle il appartenait.

On dégagea premièrement un assez grand nombre de groupes et de sous-groupes d'objets qu'on répartit en tas autour du palais.

L'observation constante des arrivages d'objets les plus divers permit rapidement de les distinguer en deux catégories seulement: les objets 'creux', les objets 'pleins'.

Deux énormes empilements hétéroclites se dressaient à présent aux alentours de la résidence impériale. La montagne de choses réputées creuses paraissait plus volumineuse que sa voisine: l'une semblait pouvoir contenir l'autre.

Les observateurs profitaient aussi de la courte durée pendant laquelle chaque chose était isolée pour l'affubler d'une sorte de titre, qui était censé l'identifier à jamais.

L'on fut tenté, d'abord, de nommer les choses par leur nom, suivi d'un chiffre: chapeau 1, chapeau 2, chapeau 3, chapeau 4, chapeau 5, chapeau 6, ...; mais la quantité de chiffres rendit vite cette méthode inadéquate. On eut donc recours à la métaphore pour désigner les moindres particularités: couvreur, boulet, crâneur, plateau, croissance, ombreur, trou... Mais cette pratique épuisa vite l'imagination de ceux qui l'exerçaient: les termes manquaient pour nommer les choses, qui affluaient sans cesse. On utilisa donc des groupes de mots et même des phrases entières.

Cette entreprise de tout qualifier retardait considérablement les progrès de l'inventaire; c'est pourquoi on associa finalement des expressions abstraites ou insignifiantes aux objets qui apparaissaient continuellement, sans plus se soucier d'une hypothétique nécessité conceptuelle ou poétique: Rbo, Elg, oucta, Imessi, sonks, tchiku, Rnanr...

L'empereur ne se contenta pas de cette gigantesque série d'objets, qui déjà formait deux tas bien plus gros que le palais lui même. Les maisons furent démontées et les gens se dépouillèrent de leurs vêtements pour venir grossir encore l'amoncellement énorme de tout ce qui avait été ratissé sur l'île.

On suggéra ensuite de se mettre en quête de la moindre chose qui ne fut pas vivante. On vit ainsi chacun collectant les cailloux et le bois mort, creusant la terre afin d'en extraire les éléments de tout être inanimé...

D'interminables discussions avaient lieu, souvent, pour décider le statut de telle pelote de ficelle par exemple: pleine ou creuse?

Une véritable catastrophe mit fin à ces atermoiements: l'immense tas d'objets 'creux' s'écroula soudainement sur son vis à vis. Dès lors on changea de tactique: on chercha à réunir, à emboîter les pleins et les vides, pour former une sorte d'objet nouveau, issu de la contraction de ses qualités contradictoires. Ces assemblages étaient ensuite nommés par une sorte de borborygme hasardeux, plus proche du bruit que du mot.

Le Japon entier fut ainsi mobilisé pendant les 25 années que dura cet infini dénombrement.

Lorsqu'on se décida enfin à interroger Mikkaddo sur la raison de cette obsessionnelle et très encombrante nécessité de tout rassembler et de tout nommer, on ne le trouva plus, le palais impérial avait disparu, recouvert sous la multitude figée. On ne distinguait rien qu'un amas informe de choses inanimées, qui contrastait singulièrement avec l'activité humaine aux alentours.

Michel François - Bruxelles, été 1990.

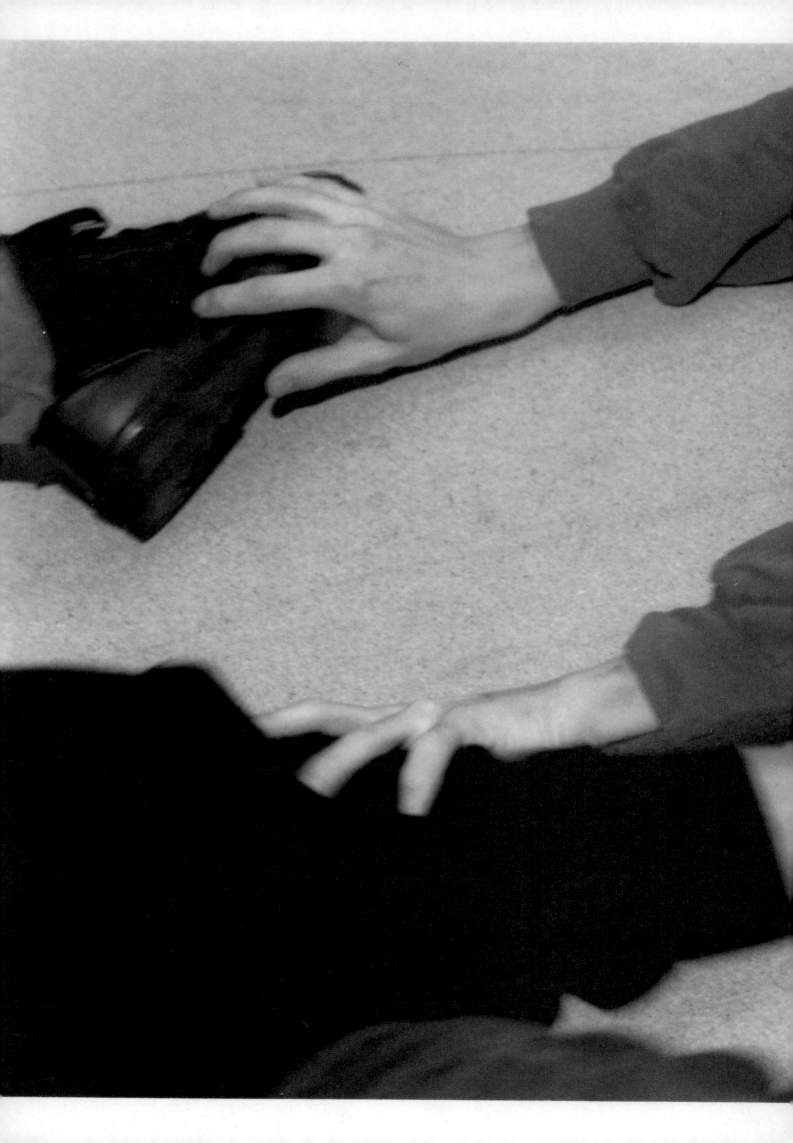

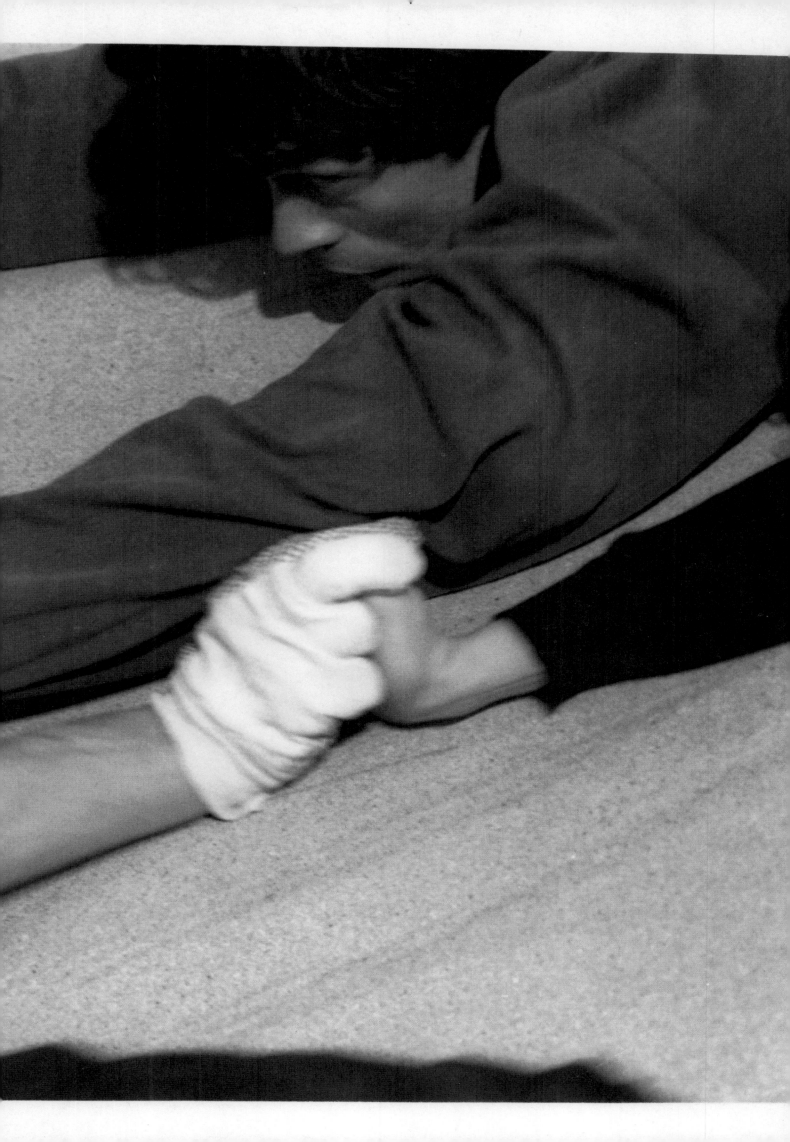

23 JUNE 2016

A letter or a postcard, who knows. Backstage I assimilate an archive that willingly confuses mountain with fountain. I mix it with air. And with wind, which belongs to another choreographic reasoning closer to vocal exercises. The time when we read *Tombeau pour New York* and the dance studio glided above Brussels. I knew the door code by heart. I remembered this combination of four numbers years later. One evening we were stuck in the lift after closing up. Our only food, half a banana, belonging to Stefan. Who looked at us half-raw half-cooked carrying across his chest a leather bag. Hardly time to ramble. To highlight a few stanzas of very French poetry. The sponge like the orange, read Pierre to Eugène, who discovered in Belgium the properties of the vacuum cleaner in his country house. Fountain. A bucket of water in which I soaked the mop. With which I wipe the dance mat to preserve the skin of my crawling colleagues. Midday strikes Thibault comes back to us from London with a pearl-white fabric in his hands that came from the packaging. Is it a dove, this purely evanescent thing absolutely alive, which breathes, which moves like we move and breathe? Air, he said, of the square of fabric that his delicateness attached with a transparent ribbon to Celia's body. On the spot the square changes and becomes a suit. Fishing line to keep it on the shoulders and it's done. Celia attired thus and with the care of a nurse that we know sticks on a surgical bandage to protect the spot. Beauty spot on her stomach that we reveal further on. On the stage where we don't completely undress her modesty. At this time, Pierre was forty years old. In the mornings, he ran all around the Parc du Forest. Someone saw him. Someone told us that Pierre played tennis with this slender guy who answered to the name of Jesus. Without making Pierre pray, squeezed half a grapefruit and set us a training session based on jumps. Daily rosary of jumps. Ah, mountain. My calves remained. Is it a down to earth story, this epoch of domestic objects by dancing? We climb, hang on, we bang in the nail. To foil gravity, Stefan throws in the air a blanket of museum aesthetic. A grey blanket that is not found in our houses. It turns. It turns flat. How does he do it? We soon discover that his father is a magician. It's the same. The son never raises his voice above the symbolic tone of the private interview as long as the German language that he pronounces in French gives him the effect of having gravel in his mouth. Aurélien, who is lodging with me, uses my Italian cotton towel woven with fringes used as a tea towel. It's not possible, I say, in order to free myself from so many grease stains. If you do French cooking on my dowry I will never get married. That said the same cook playing the accordion bursting into laughter. How we laughed in Paris at the liberation. Ah, mountain. Going in to the left of the production offices, we glimpse Tarquin's profile behind a notice which says: Do not throw peanuts please. In front of the mountain Pierre, site director, asks us to divide the

full and the empty, please we need to transform all that into a fountain. And
it flows. He is influenced by the American trends, which tend to lighten us of
all this cumbersome material. Contemporary dance becomes a museum. We don't
yet have the time to think about the museums of the future. Come on, let's dive
into the pile to fix his count of objects, he says. We obey, like in Iraq we push
our heads, the first we blend, all the full, all the empty, bumping up against
all the same, the enigma of the bicycle handlebar. Is it full? Is it empty?
Asks studiously Xavier at Stefan's dance so completely elastic. Because of this
he just escapes the hard tasks we others get lumbered with. We sign up for the
army. Celia agrees. She takes as a score, her toothache. I pick out things from
the pile with a marked preference for the full because we never know. Better
not to trust the empty I say to myself. To grab from the pile all relevant
object of a sufficiently dense corporal mass. The mountain. The collection of
LP records. The barrel. The enormous roll of string. Empathy and affinity come
into play early on. On certain days Michel is François who is followed by his
past in the studio. Careful! He's coming! With François, we smash up the place
by order. A pile of plates with a hammer. Simon follows him with his unusual
awkwardness. Anvil my body squashed. Weigh myself. Only one cobblestone within
reach. You should have been a soldier in a previous life Pierre tells me. What
is my present life I say and become the office desk that Stefan is moving. Bang.
Bang. In this section the costume of toothache is a pair of trousers with a
red waistcoat. It's new, she says, usually I dress in green. That said, she
eats her daily banana for the additional potassium. Ascension from one day to
the next when Pierre announced the project with the sloping stage. Once made
with the motor that goes with it, we get used to it. During this time I have
maintained a family connection with the drop of rainwater that clings to the
windowpane. With the tear that traces a path down my cheek until I come back
into circulation. By the mouth. Sunday we go for brunch at Ida's house who
keeps a lighted candle on the chimneypiece in the middle of the day. And an
amaryllis flower. The rest of the week Harry learns the nuances of Pierre's
language. I brush my teeth. I brush my teeth. I brush my teeth, he repeats. When
he throws himself stomach to stomach on me he is extraordinarily light, he has
the texture of a foam mattress. It's perhaps like that that this should finally
be. After all, he too comes from London. Waistcoat and grey fitted trousers don't
protect me from the blows, my body is covered in bruises from my love with the
material. Rue de Parme, I am hunched in front of the gas heater. Tiredness I
don't think about, I sleep like a log. Antoine tells me that we can see the
results of the races on the video again. But what the dancers uses shuts up.
It can only be sweat. These five dancers. Five drops perspire from the page.
Fountain. Oh, mountain. That will make Pierre's book.

1996:   Creation of *De l'air et du vent*
2010:   New version of *De l'air et du vent* with Collectif Loge 22
2011:   Rerun of *De l'air et du vent*

DE L'AIR ET DU VENT
Choreography: Pierre Droulers
With: Carlos De Haro, Stefan Dreher, Thomas Hauert, Celia Hope Simpson, Martine Lunshof
Choreography, assistant: Barbara Manzetti
Music: Jean-Philippe Rameau, Luciano Berio, György Kurtág
Soundtrack: Philippe Cam
Artistic collaboration: Ann Veronica Janssens
Costumes: Thibault Vancraenenbroeck
Lighting: Jim Clayburgh
First performance: 6 September 1996, Festival La Bâtie, Geneva
Co-production: Charleroi/Danses, La Bâtie, Festival de Genève - Forum Meyrin, Dans in Kortrijk

DE L'AIR ET DU VENT (revival)
Choreography: Pierre Droulers
Artistic collaboration: Collectif Loge 22
With: Julien Monty, Marie Goudot, Michaël Pomero, Thomas Michaux, Cécile Laloy, Martine Lunshof, Nathan Freyermuth
First performance: 25 November 2010, La Raffinerie, Brussels
Production: Charleroi Danses
Co-production: Collectif Loge 22

DE L'AIR ET DU VENT (rerun)
Choreography: Pierre Droulers
With: Michel Yang, Katrien Vandergooten, Yoann Boyer, Stefan Dreher, Peter Savel
Costumes: Chevalier-Masson
First performance: 10 May 2011, Festival Évidanse, Belfort
Production: Charleroi/Danses. Aided by Wallonie-Bruxelles Internationale
and Wallonie-Bruxelles Théâtre/Danse. Supported by Arcadi

DE L'AIR ET DU VENT
1996

NOUS VOYONS PLUS INTENSÉMENT

PAR UNE LUMIÈRE QUI DISPARAÎT

QUE PAR UNE MÈCHE QUI DEMEURE.

QUELQUE CHOSE DANS L'ENVOL

CLARIFIE LA VUE

ET MAGNIFIE LES LUEURS.

EMILY DICKINSON

Toute chose qui viendra est ancienne
Choisis une autre amie que cette folie.
                    Prépare-toi
à rester à l'écart.

Adonis, 'Mémoire du vent', *Poèmes 1957-1990*

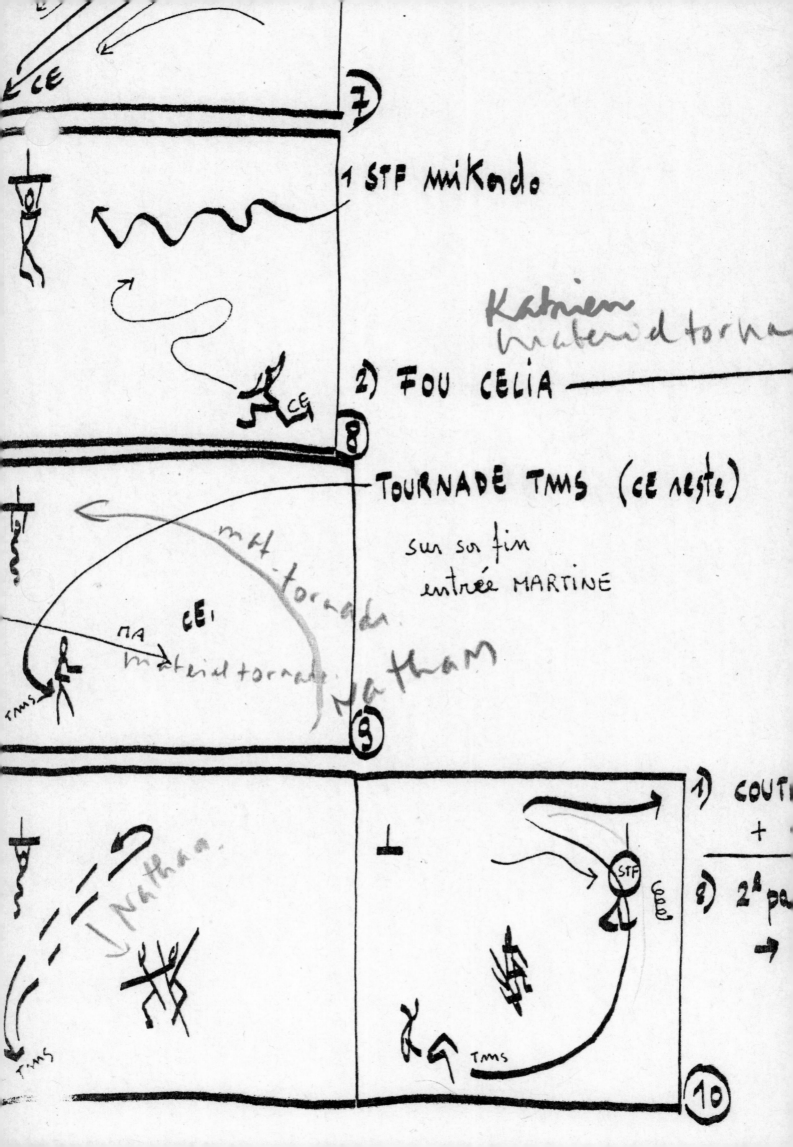

⑦

1 STF miKado

Katrien
matériel torna

2) FOU CELIA ——————

⑧

TOURNADE TMS (CE reste)

sur sa fin
entrée MARTINE

mat-tornade

MA   CE1
matériel tornade

Nathan

⑨

Nathan

1) COUT
+

3) 2ª pa
→

STF

CE1

TMS

⑩

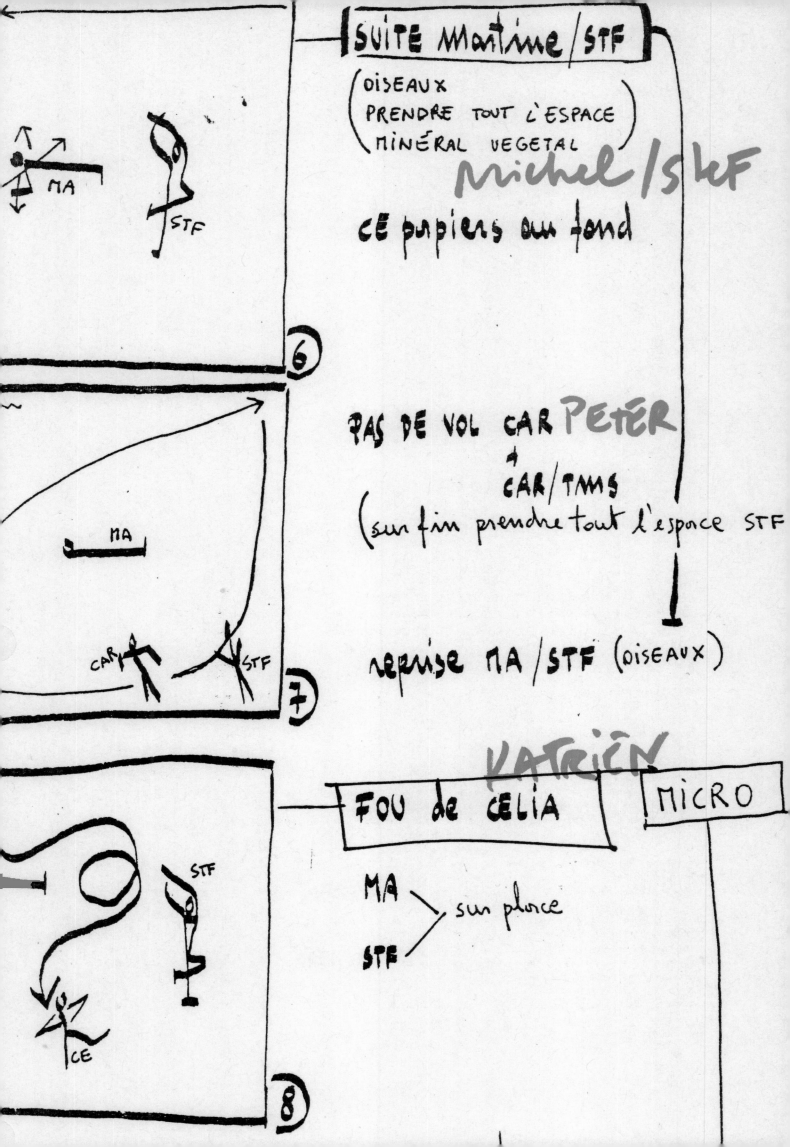

SUITE Martine/STF

(OISEAUX
PRENDRE TOUT L'ESPACE)
MINÉRAL VÉGÉTAL)

Michel / stf

CE papiers au fond

⑥

PAS DE VOL CAR PETER
+
CAR/TMS
(sur fin prendre tout l'espace STF

reprise MA/STF (OISEAUX)

⑦

KATRIEN

FOU de CELIA | MICRO

MA ⟩ sur place
STF

⑧

MA

STF

CAR   STF

STF

CE

1996:   Creation of *Les Beaux Jours*
1997:   Creation of *Petites Formes*
2011:   New version of *Les Beaux Jours*
2017:   New version of *Les Beaux Jours*

LES BEAUX JOURS
Choreography: Pierre Droulers
With: Tijen Lawton
Lighting: Jim Clayburgh
Costumes: Thibault Vancraenenbroeck
Co-production: Dans in Kortrijk

PETITES FORMES (8 solos for 4 dancers)
Choreography: Pierre Droulers and the dancers
With: Stefan Dreher (*Zoo Walking with Rider* and *Gehen*), Thomas Hauert (*Personne* and *Hoboken dans*), Tijen Lawton (*Les Beaux Jours* and *Je n'ai jamais parlé*), Celia Hope Simpson (*Rousse* and *4 heures du matin*)
Music: Tielman Susato (*Dansereye 1551*), Luciano Berio (*Rousse*), Heinz Holliger (*Personne*)
Costumes: Patrick Pitschon, Thibault Vancraenenbroeck
Lighting: Jim Clayburgh
Set design: Simon Siegmann (*Personne*)
First performance: 1997, Kortrijk
Co-production: Dans in Kortrijk, Charleroi/Danses, Les Brigittines, La Bellone, De Beweging

LES BEAUX JOURS (2011 broadcast)
Choreography: Pierre Droulers
With: Katrien Vandergooten
First performance: 15 November 2011, BPS22, Biennale de Charleroi Danses, Charleroi
Production: Charleroi/Danses

LES BEAUX JOURS (2017 broadcast)
Choreography: Pierre Droulers
With: Malika Djardi

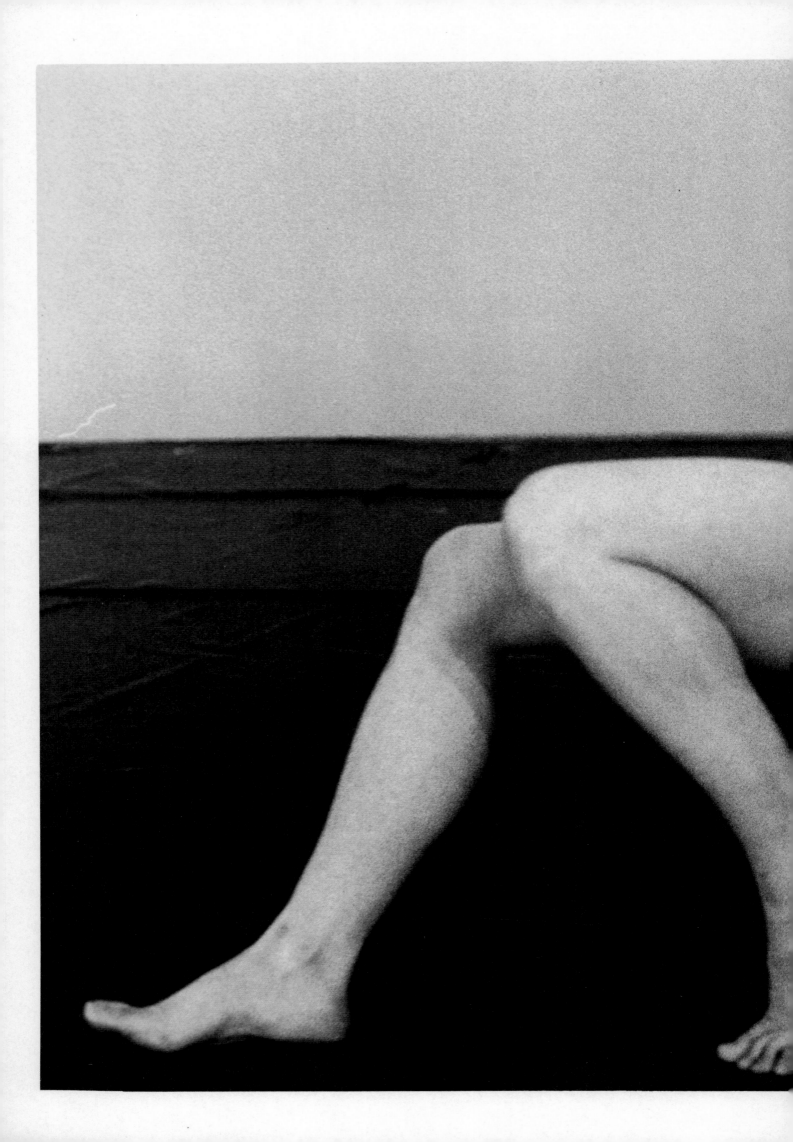

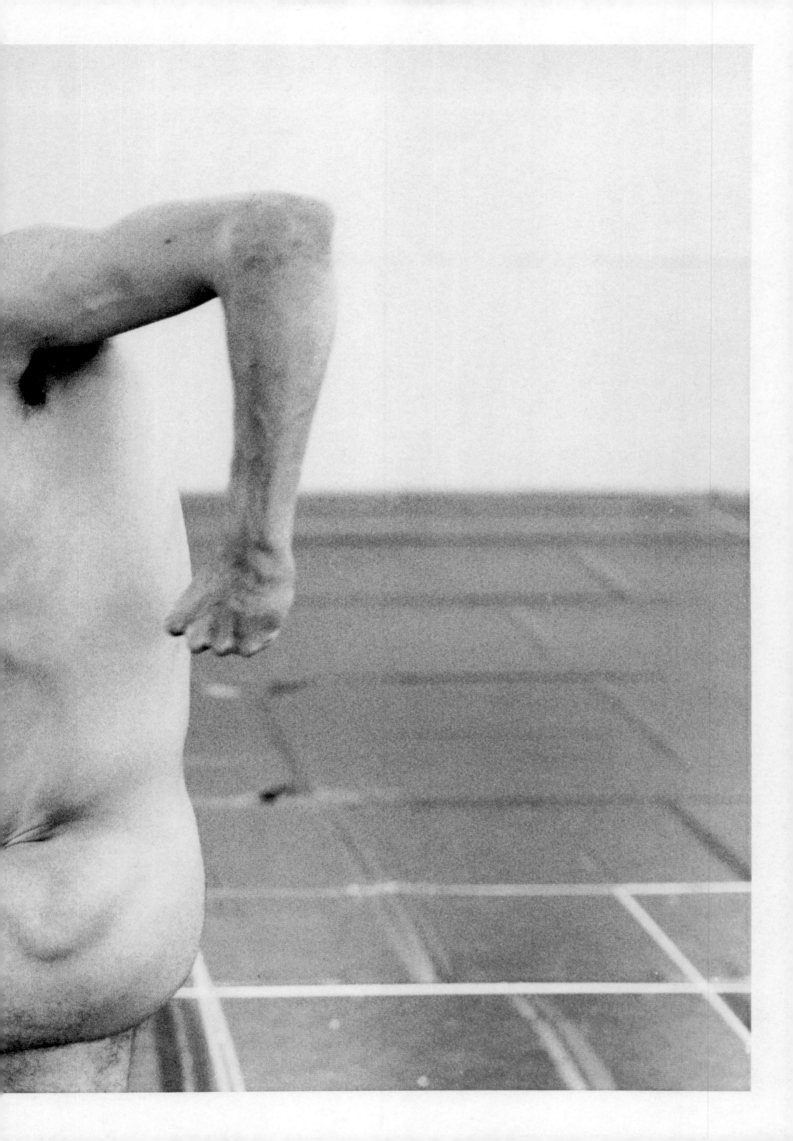

1998:   Creation of *Multum in Parvo*

MULTUM IN PARVO
Choreography: Pierre Droulers
With: Manolo Canteria, Aurélien Desclozeaux, Éléonore Didier, Éric Domeneghetty, Stefan Dreher, Julien Faure, Serge Finschi, Lisa Gunstone, Thomas Hauert, Harold Henning, Celia Hope Simpson, Silke Hundertmark, Anne Huwaert, Inken Landskröner, Tijen Lawton, Martine Lunshof, Monica Marti, Esteban Pena Villagran, Carole Perdereau, Karine Ponties, Anabel Schellekens, Harry Theaker, Li Ping Ting, Tamarah Tossey, Silvia Ubieta
Soundtrack: Philippe Cam
Music: Maurizio Kagel, György Kurtág, György Ligeti, Johann Sebastian Bach
Set design: Simon Siegmann
Set design, assistant: Alexandre Chinon
Artistic direction, assistant: Frauke Furthmann
Lighting: Jim Clayburgh
Costumes: Nathalie Douxfils, Veerle Van den Wouwer
Publication: Tarquin Billiet, Sofie Kokaj, Hans Theys
First performance: 25 May 1998, Théâtre Les Tanneurs, Kunstenfestivaldesarts, Brussels
Co-production: Charleroi/Danses, Kunstenfestivaldesarts

alexandre
anabel
anne
aurélien
carole
celia
déborah
éléonore
éric
esteban
estelle
frauke
harold
inken
jim
julien
karine
li-ping
lisa
manolo
martine
monica
nathalie
philippa
philippe b.
philippe c.
philippe v.
pierre
ruth
serge
silke
silvia
simon
sofie
stefan
tamarah
tarquin
thomas
tijen
veerle

MULTUM IN
PARVO
1998

alexandre
anabel
anne
aurélien
carole
celia
déborah
éléonore
éric
esteban
estelle
frauke
harold
inken
jie
julien
karine
li-ping
lisa
manolo
martine
monica
nathalie
philippe
philippe b.
philippe o.
philippe v.
pierre
ruth
serge
silke
silvia
simon
sofie
stefan
tamarah
tarquin
thomas
tijen
veerle

MULTUM

S

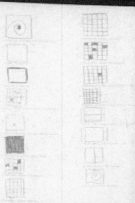

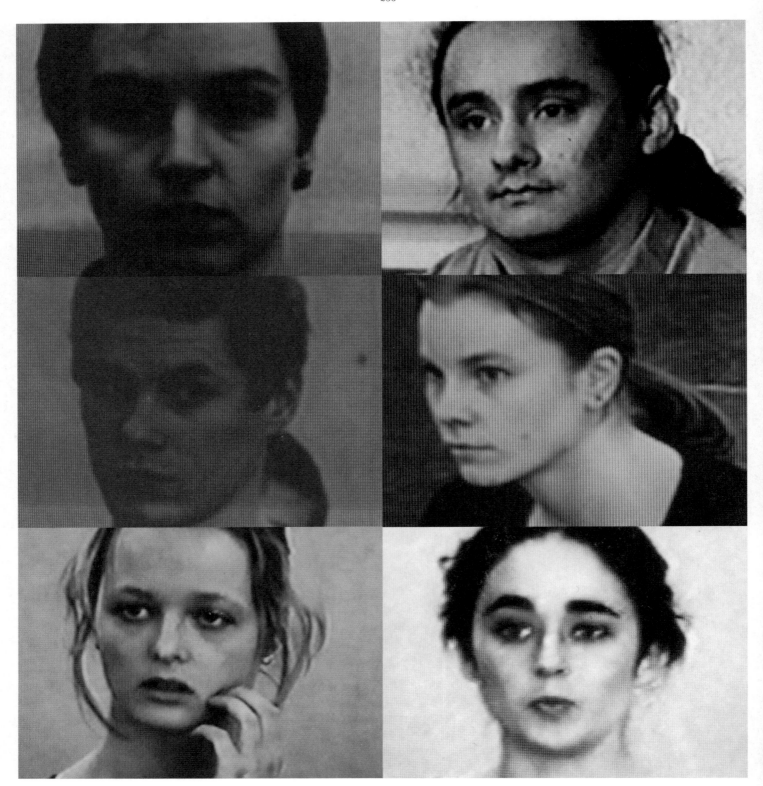

Je suis moi. Et moi, c'est moi. Je suis moi.
Je suis ici. Je suis quelque chose. Je suis

quelqu'un. J'arrive haut, très haut. Je peux
sauter, gambader, courir vite comme le vent.
Je peux crier fort, marcher rapidement.
Je sais me battre.

Multum in Parvo

Un soir, tout le monde est tombé.

Le sol était en béton recouvert de carton, très glissant. Malgré toutes les tentatives d'y répandre du coca-cola pour le rendre plus adhérent, ce sont les danseurs qui s'y sont répandus.

Il y avait une course dans la pièce, une sorte de tourbillon où quasi tout le groupe courrait en rond.

J'étais au centre, immobile, les bras en croix et couvert de petits cadeaux.

Je ne voyais pas grand-chose, mais j'entendais tout, des corps se rétamer par terre les uns après les autres, comme s'ils se poursuivaient sur du verglas avec des semelles lisses.

C'était violent et ça faisait mal.

Pour un spectacle dont le thème était l'herbe, on réalisait là, malgré et en dépit de nous, une authentique scène de moisson.

Harold Henning – 1 Juillet 2011

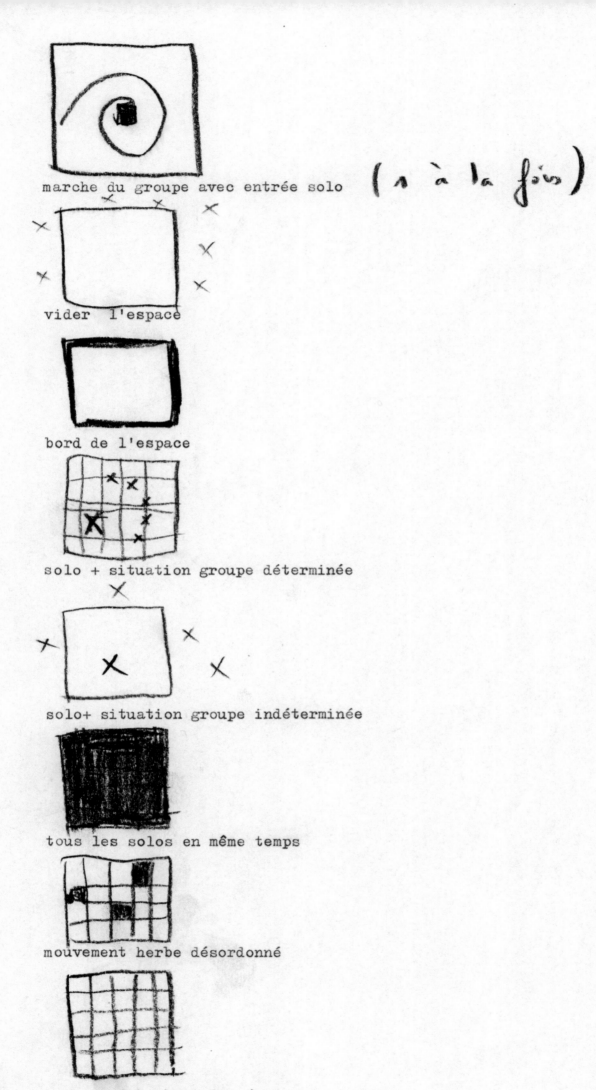

marche du groupe avec entrée solo   (1 à la fois)

vider l'espace

bord de l'espace

solo + situation groupe déterminée

solo+ situation groupe indéterminée

tous les solos en même temps

mouvement herbe désordonné

mouvement herbe ordonné

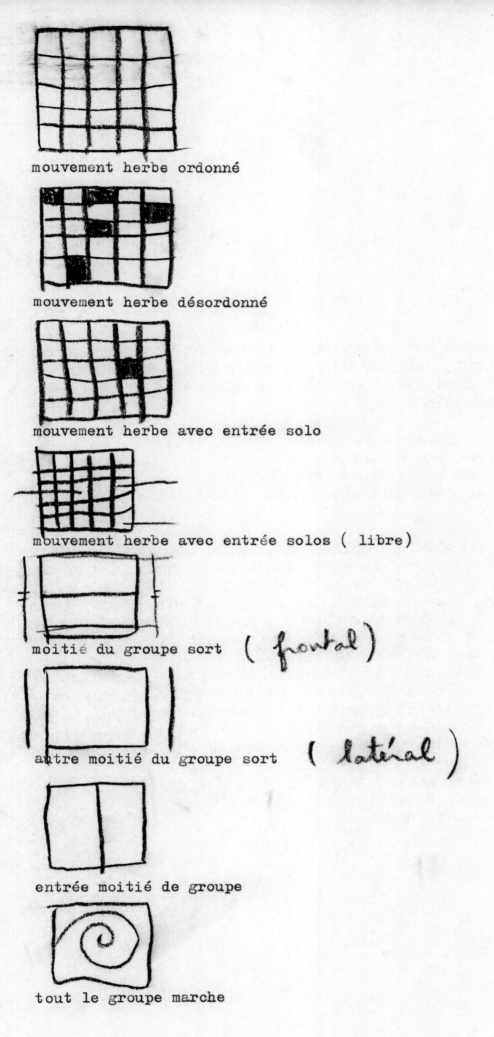

mouvement herbe ordonné

mouvement herbe désordonné

mouvement herbe avec entrée solo

mouvement herbe avec entrée solos (libre)

moitié du groupe sort (frontal)

autre moitié du groupe sort (latéral)

entrée moitié de groupe

tout le groupe marche

Multum in parvo

Vingt cinq solos, au départ de l'herbe. Qui prennent forme, qui s'épuisent à travers champs. Chacun trouve en effet quatre états à traverser où il va éprouver sa spécificité unique et solitaire, en prendre la mesure, jouer sa peau dans et devant la multitude:

un champs d'herbe; seul parmi les autres
un champs de tir; seul face aux autres
un champ de foire; les autres, à traverser
un champs nouveau; retour au champ d'herbe, après l'épreuve des possibles, si possible.

Chacun propose. On regarde, on parle. Puis un autre, une autre. Ce sont des rencontres. Fouiller, revisiter, défendre, observer, démonter, expliquer dans ces moments en commun voilà ce qu'ils font. Il y a des questions d'espace, d'image, de texture; pourquoi alors devant, pourquoi vers l'arrière maintenant, pourquoi ceci plutôt que cela. Mais aussi que sont ces champs, où y suis-je, où y sommes-nous? Va-t-on s'y rallier et comment. Tous sont toujours différents. Qui du théâtre, qui de la danse, qui de nulle part. L'un d'ici, l'autre de là-bas etc...Il faut du temps pour y éprouver sa mythologie personnelle.
N'être, qu'une herbe. Faire à la fin l'herbier des mythologies personnelles.
Ils sont aussi très souvent tous ensemble, à travers champs. Il y a peut-être une communauté.
Des gens sont venus filmer. Certains viennent avec un objet ou un écrit, ils ne dansent pas.
A la fin des ateliers, le public vient aussi. "Voir si j'y suis".
Et puis on recommence. Ailleurs.
Comment déjà, y-est-elle, l'herbe?

Tarquin Billiet

Paris, le 31 mai 1998,

Pierre,

Il était temps que se fragmente enfin le discours frontalier pour laisser l'éboulement
évoquer sa propre figure.Je croisai Kitty Kortes Lynch après « Multum » et lui confiai qu'il
s'agissait pour moi ici d'une géométrie sociétale,c'est à dire où la constante réside dans
le premier terme.J'y ai vu le vitrail de notre aube, inondé de réel qui dé-place pour ré-
agencer , qui ne peut subsister que dans le déplacement.Il faudra donc apprendre (ce
que tu esquisses superbement) à ne pas occuper un territoire tout juste conquis, mais à
le réchauffer pour en faciliter la liquidation.Il faudra laisser une trace pour qu'un indice
de rencontre subsiste en dépit des fluctuations.Réchauffer la planète aurait dû être le
projet conscient de l'humanité.
Ce qui m'a également rassuré (car toute expérience spectative est désormais placée
sous le spectre d'une mise en scène de l'arrogance) c'est de voir qu'une théorie peut
s'initier dans l'événement de l'acte.C'est cette découverte qui demeure.
Par théorie je pense en premier lieu à un système qui se découvre dans le temps de son
affrontement au réel:une hypothèse déjà indispensable qui dit que le temps de la
pensée traverse l'idée de sorte à ne plus instaurer de "faille" entre l'acte et sa source.
«Multum in Parvo» est donc de l'art d'aujourd'hui:répondre dans la singularisation d'un
potentiel de multiplicité.

La "pauvreté" n'est donc guère synonyme de dénuement mais délestage de
l'usurpation.Elle se débarrasse de ce qui encombre et dégrade, et, comble du paradoxe,
cette pauvreté n'est jamais acquise,elle exige que l'on y porte un soin extrême,c'est une
ouverture abyssale qui méprise l'accession et exalte le creuset.
S'y fait jour une transparence qui accompagne le labeur de l'extraction jusqu'à effleurer
la parol objectale:celle-ci ne sera rompue que pour témoigner d'une transparence
transmissible.
Connais-tu cet aphorisme de René Char: « à chaque effondrement des preuves, le poète
répond par une salve d'avenir».

A bientôt.

Alain Franco

Rue de Ménilmontant 157
75020   Paris
Tel/Fax 01.43.61.30.91
e-mail: FRANCO1848@aol.com

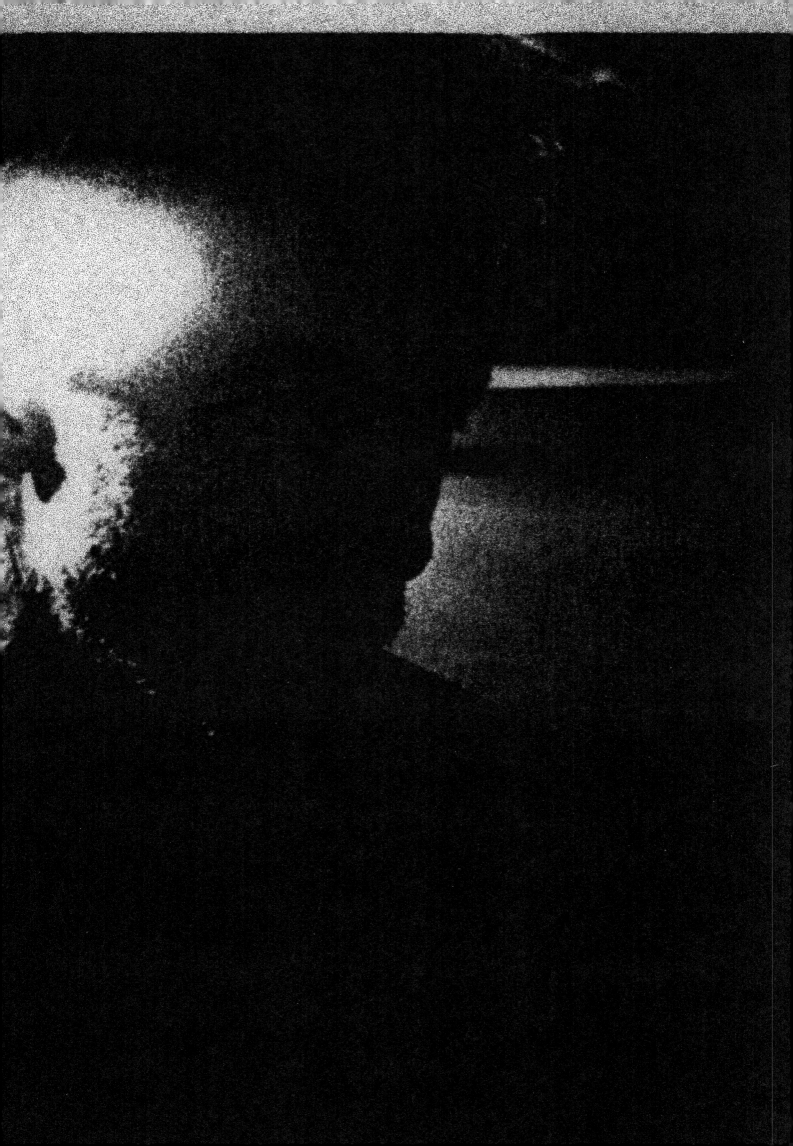

TO PIERRE, FROM MEMORY...

It began like this: I didn't have any work, Pierre Droulers didn't have an
administrator. We didn't know each other. We were thrown together. And we
were off: I turned up with my little satchel and freshly sharpened pencils
on a lovely April morning in 1993, rue du Mail, in Ixelles, in the deserted
offices of the company.

We quickly got on well, Pierre and I. We discussed everything, crucial
questions for the company first of all. Of the possible resumption of *Jamais de
l'abîme* (the dancers' tour, the organisation – a well-known tune), hesitating
(already) between a possible resumption and an inevitable abandonment. As we
talked about a new project (*Mountain/Fountain*), we explored the past, the
history of his work, his career, a little of his life. The conversation
wandered at length over the small and large details of life, our physical
and spiritual sustenance ('pâté and a glass of red', a 'small salad' at
midday, Beckett, Joyce, Leiris, cars, Archie Shepp, Braxton, Lacy, Purcell,
motorbikes, the south, Belgium, Cassavetes, Bresson, Godard...).

Very quickly, we had an exuberant profusion of ideas, of projects,
aspirations, desires – from which we had to choose, to sort out, to
decide. Both of us having greedily shopped at the Spanish and Portuguese
delicatessens where, hung from the ceiling, were dozens of appetising
hams, we consoled ourselves with the image of having to make choices, by
persuading ourselves that what was provisionally left to one side remained
nearby, maturing slowly in our own imaginary delicatessen of hanging hams.

Officially my role was 'administrator'. That's to say the money, the
subsidies, the co-productions, the tours, the washing-up, wiping the dance
studio mat (water + vinegar I discovered), the printer's ink cartridges, the
toilet paper, the schedulers, the co-producers, the Ministry of Performing
Arts, the caretaker, the plumber, the bank transfers, filling up the fridge,
filling up the stapler, negotiating the bank credit. The money: not to sit on
it. Lift up your behind, one buttock or the other, sometimes both, in order
to find some. To let go sometimes in order to dream, to create, to invent –
often reshuffling the cards. To scrupulously watch over the piles and bundles
of 'cleaning money' like a good family patriarch. Like a naughty boy to
turn on the blower that scatters this confounded pile during the exuberance
of a change of direction. To set sail but, as the show got closer, end up
coasting closer to land: a squaring of the circle which, with Pierre, we
enjoyed – not without some passing storms.

Most of the time we 'administrated' together. We weren't holding the
same ends of the string of course, but we always managed to join the two
ends together. I liked his work, his universe. I felt at home there – and,
also, we got on well. But, according to Pierre, for two people to work well

together, you need to be three. And actually, that was proven true, this need for an association with a third person – actually, always a woman. This one had, among other things, the difficult task, thankless – tearful as well when Pierre got into a bad temper – to look after the tours. The memory of the tours of *Remains* with Steve Lacy, as a duo, returns again and again obsessively (and with a keen nostalgia): 'we set off by car with everything we needed stowed in the boot: Steve's sax, the costumes, one or two accessories, and off we went'. (Pierre's culinary comparison for this ideal tour was another mantra: 'A little goat's cheese, an olive, a piece of bread and a small glass of red.')

In reality, the work with Pierre can't be classified. La Compagnie Droulers is a chaotic household. But a noble house. Not a castle, however. You need to be let in, nevertheless. To be anointed, a bit, even so. In fact, after a while I often began my sentences with 'I'm only a moronic administrator, but…' Even I was reminded of my responsibilities, as we shuffled through books, precious texts, of the memories of shows, of films, of musical pleasures, of slap-up meals, of journeys, of meetings – we ranged across the horizon, we pondered on the details, with pleasure.

When we met, Pierre thought I was more into books, magazines, writing. However, he had seen my CV. He no doubt read it 'inattentively'. He didn't give a damn about CVs. For him there were only meetings. He crossed paths with people. And then there were those who fell into the ditch. It was like that.

I didn't really know anything about dance. At performances I was spellbound to see what could be said without words. Given my personal taste, which had already directed me towards music, it stimulated an extraordinary relief in me – this alternative to chit-chat, even to language, this other way – this often dazzling shortcut. Given the lack of words, I was intrigued and surprised, however, to feel with such strength a profound resonance, even when I was watching rehearsals, and later in the performances. Pierre's performances weren't the first that I saw, but were the first that I saw close up. It hit me in the gut. Sometimes like a mirror, a familiar world certainly, intimate, poetic, with a melancholic elegance, that swung between imminent disaster and great heights, with sensuality, humour, derision, with small touches of the circus and the shadowy world of Méliès and the aristocratic style of his Arte Povera period.

Mountain/Fountain is a work about liquidation, interpreted as liquefaction, fluidification: a tabula rasa, but which in its movement flows like a river towards the sea. I liked that. I wanted to see that.

I wanted to see that in performance. As Pierre would take on the work, I would accompany him, as a presence. How would everything take shape if we managed to achieve it? That resonated with me. I could clearly see Pierre's desires. I was happy to accompany him, to go into battle together – for my part I only ever dealt with my obsessions by sorting out my administrative paperwork, or at least my books and photos, not as an artist.

At this point, Pierre had almost twenty years of work behind him. We moved into a new studio in the rue des Ateliers. A magnificent space: sunrise in the studio in the east, sunset in the west, on the side of the offices towards the exit. A whole universe. We brought in all the significant objects, and kept them there. In fact, everyone was re-evaluated, and reviewed as well. We find that in *Mountain/Fountain*. The dancers could use it like a treasure chest, using a charm, a score, in the performance. At the same time, Pierre threw the dice again, and brought in his friend Michel François, sculptor and visual artist. I think this was the first time he went in this particular direction.

Michel introduced his works; Pierre and the dancers used them. We kept them or we put them aside. We used them again. We discarded them. It worked as simply as that. Small metal balls, a hanging cardboard ball (Celia), a bag of confetti (Harry), and his videos front of stage, shown on a small simple Barco monitor. Pierre and Michel had designed a simple stage. Just a flat L shape, the vertical partition at the back tilted at the end of the performance, like the ending of an hour-long meandering dream. A rectangular surface that was also the framework from which the dancers and Pierre, who was also a dancer, made their entrances and exits.

It was a good working method for the staging: but Michel enjoyed getting it re-explained to him as often as possible – 'what's my role in fact?', 'what do you want from me exactly?' – 'and me, what am I playing at?' Actually, it worked out as smoothly as it could. Michel was, as is normal, a tortured being who was like a charming pain in the neck, and we were asked, when he frequently doubted himself, to formally grant him a moment to discuss things. Which wasn't any use, because there was nothing to sort out. His work blended in with the general dynamic, in the writing, in the temporality of the performance. We set him going, and he joined in with the overall framework of the writing. Michel's works remained in the studio for a long time, along with his crates and video cassettes – despite the fact that from the beginning of our work together we teased him by saying that we would quietly sell his work to finance the company's projects. With every answer to the eternal question 'what's my status?', we almost succeeded in making him believe that we had actually only hired him in order to swindle him.

Going from the office via the studio to take a break, I went into another world. I saw the dancers warming up in complete silence, just a few faint sounds of fabric brushing the ground, the sounds of breathing, blank looks, sometimes strangely stretched out on their backs, their winding limbs folded above them. I ended up by saying: 'You've really got a strange job.' Funny creatures, dancers… a nomadic tribe, said Pierre. Backpack, a bundle of possessions, they set up camp anywhere. 'On the road.' They stop off at each other's houses, from one town to the next, 'my home is your home', sleeping standing up if necessary. An audition here, an audition there… like the seasonal workers for the grape harvest or olive picking: the seasonal workers of contemporary dance. At the auditions that we held in Paris, Pierre told me of his horror of these moments of choice – he could never make up his mind to dismiss a member of the 'tribe', of the community (bizarrely, it fell to the 'administrator' to call the dancers after the auditions).

Pierre liked noise, sound and, as much as music, the sound of the voice. It's in his performances. Particularly in *Mountain/Fountain*, *De l'air et du vent*, and others, later on. In music, Pierre's love of blankness is the respect given to silence, listening to what emerges. For Michel François's videos, we had a moment of great technological excitement ('everything on the backdrop', imposing, vast, the images used full frame. 'How can we do it – how much does it cost – where can we find this equipment?'). We were all occupied with the sound. Playing with sound amplification, footsteps, sighs, fixing an arrangement of sensors and filling the stage with them. And, ultimately, you just had to listen. Metal balls rolling around on the stage like the sound of a storm, the static crackle of Michel François's videos, the drumming on a long tree trunk, the sound of tinplate boxes, chalk being scraped across the floor (Barbara), footsteps, races, bodies falling, delicate brushing sounds, the changing rhythm of the dancers' breathing, banging – a whole score actually born from movement, from the manipulation of objects, from the life of the stage, and which created density and depth.

Throwing music in like this was like fishing with dynamite. That said, the detonation of Thierry De Mey's piano pieces was intentional. He delicately perked up the movement and the energy of *Mountain/Fountain*. Musically, the intermediate contribution was the piece by Baudouin de Jaer and Fabian Fiorini. In *Jamais de l'abîme*, Baudouin had composed music that Pierre still remembered. Baudouin and Fabian therefore turned up at the studio the day after one of their ritual compositions, made up of songs and music performed at night under a full moon among the trees in the Sonian Forest. Completely crazy. They came back some time later with a small melody like a music box, fragile and dislocated, a prepared piano piece with notes, sounds and noise – which was used, here and there in *Mountain/Fountain*. And for the rest, all the sound came from the action, or from the stillness, in silence. This time, using the art of trout-fishing applied to sound.

For *De l'air et du vent* I looked for music, for pieces of music. I put together a small selection to choose from, as we do with the Droulers method. For the rest, Pierre continued in the same vein as *Mountain/Fountain*. Sounds of cables dragged across the stage, dropping onto enormous bulging inflated cardboard cushions, hissing as they deflated, little tinklings here and there, the silent cry of Stefan Dreher, miming in slow motion the roaring lion from Metro-Goldwyn-Mayer. From my extensive but discrete selection, Kurtág and Berio remained in play. From small string motifs, borrowed and placed in shadowy moments, to lightly sketched elegantly desolate moods, moving on to discrete melancholy places on the edge of disillusionment.

The real fishing with dynamite here was the sudden arrival of the Rameau melody that burst in two-thirds of the way into the performance. Very unobtrusively, the score began with wind noise, blending in perfectly with the soundtrack that preceded it, no doubt a small wind machine of the period. Then it suddenly took off, in a whirl of wind and trees, ethereal, irresistible, swirling, like a splattering of tone and colour across a black and white performance – simultaneously preposterous and absolutely right.

We also took one step further in *Mountain/Fountain* by working with Philippe Cam on an electronic score. Pierre asked him again and again for a 'backdrop' for the whole performance, a tracery of sound. Philippe, for his part, returned repeatedly with limited material that he then developed bit by bit through sleepless nights, which gave him a sore head ('I don't see daylight', 'I'll come more towards the end of the afternoon'). He had recycled the sounds and noises from *Mountain/Fountain*, and developed a unique linchpin of his sound: a great explosion of spiky harmonies loaded with intonations, that began pianissimo, then grew louder in faltering stages, to at last rise up like an enormous thundering wave. As for the lighting, most of the illumination was created by four super-powerful quartz lights that were languidly suspended at mid-height above the stage, under which the dancers came when they wanted to, fluttering like moths. Jim Clayburgh turned them up full at moments of musical crescendo, creating a feeling of the end of the world ('in my end is my beginning' is a favourite quotation of Pierre's). *De l'air et du vent* shows the development of a large arc that encapsulates Keaton, Beckett and Pascal

('the sole cause of man's unhappiness is that he does not know how to stay
quietly in his room' - right?) with one gesture, an incredibly long and
continuous gesture, bisected however by interruptions, changes of mood and
of energies, by repetitions, skilfully slipped in…

With Pierre's performances, 'with the participation of the dancers' is
always pointed out. There are some people who are not credited, of course.
But Pierre does not claim to work alone, nor to create by himself, nor
just with the dancers. These moments come during the composition, working
with time, images and sequences, measuring and blending the ingredients.
Professionally by necessity, as the performance gets nearer. Leaving all
the work open to everyone, I suppose it's up to him to decide when and how
to haul the net back in. That was always a preoccupation, a real topic
of discussion, the recurring question in choreography, the authorship of
performance - with the strong repeated desire to one day give shape to the
dream of working with the large numbers of the 'nomadic tribe', without
auditions, with the equal collective effort of artists working together,
like Chris Marker did in *Loin du Vietnam*, for example. With *Multum in
Parvo*, created much later for the Kunstenfestivaldesarts (1998), Pierre
wanted a poetical-political performance - in sum, made up of contributions
from each person for a performance by everyone - which would also serve
as a sort of political and aesthetic manifesto. 'A lot with little', the
translation of *Multum in Parvo* is not elegant: it's the sensitivity to
the smallest detail, the look of starkness, the absence of emphasis, the
challenge of creating a richness of meaning from a groundwork of radically
restricted artistic means. Materially as well, it was an inventive way
around the economic impossibility of producing, in the usual way, a work on
this scale and in this tone, and that only an openly collective strength of
will would make possible.

We didn't want to have a script for the performance, but a small square
volume of typewritten quotations, bound up with a simple string attached
through the corners of the square pages, gathering together the texts
that had been meticulously read, examined, discussed and used for the
performance and during the preparatory work. With this transparency, the
reader could understand who had guided us. Words from Maurice Blanchot,
Peter Handke, Luigi Nono, Gaston Bachelard, the regulations concerning
stray dogs taken from the entrance to a park, etc. - without attribution,
so that their strength came from their content and not from the reputation
of the author.

It was a hive of activity; dancers, performers, a profusion of scores,
drawings, photographs, film clips, sounds, music; set down, suggested,

removed, gathered together. Grass: it was the governing image of this
acknowledged community. The performance: a faraway meadow in the country,
which for an hour is buffeted by the wind, forms taking shape. There was
the performance, a film and an exhibition in the gallery of the Théâtre
Les Tanneurs. All this in the melting pot of Joseph Beuys's 'everyone is an
artist', but each person remaining anonymous.

As Samuel Beckett said, and he knew a bit about sobriety: 'We had a good
time.'

There were other moments. The solo performance *Les Beaux Jours*, the rerun
of *Humeurs*, the rerun of *Sames*, the *Petites Formes*, *Aventures/Nouvelles
Aventures* at the Kaaitheater, *Rappresentatione di Anima e di Corpo* at La
Monnaie, the *Parades* at La Balsamine, the *Suspension temporelle* at the
Musée d'Art Contemporain in Marseille, *Inouï*…

But I'm stopping now.

We can't talk about everything.

And yet we need to talk about everything, talk about other people as well,
all the people… Pierre, my friend, we simply had good times. All together.

2000:   Creation of *MA*
2000:   Birth of Bram Droulers

MA
Choreography: Pierre Droulers
With: Katrien Vandergooten, Stefan Dreher, Céline Perroud, Harold Henning, I-Fang Lin, Celia Hope Simpson/Lisa Gunstone
Choreography, assistant: Johanne Saunier
Music: Seth Josel, Fred Frith, Helmut Lachenmann, Microdot, Heiner Goebbels, Thelonious Monk, Yuji Oshima
Soundtrack: Alexandre Fostier
Sound design: Yuji Oshima
Lighting: Jim Clayburgh
Video: Ann Veronica Janssens, Ali Durt
Costumes: Anne Frère
Artistic inspiration: Ann Veronica Janssen, Michel François
Publications: Sofie Kokaj, Hans Theys (*Cahiers MA*)
First performance: 8 September 2000, Théâtre de Forum Meyrin, Geneva
Co-production: Brussel/Bruxelles 2000, Charleroi/Danses, Festival d'Automne Paris, Festival La Bâtie, Geneva, Théâtre de la Bastille, Paris

MA

3

Flâner

1) score source
2) score space
3) score stories

créer de
l'espace

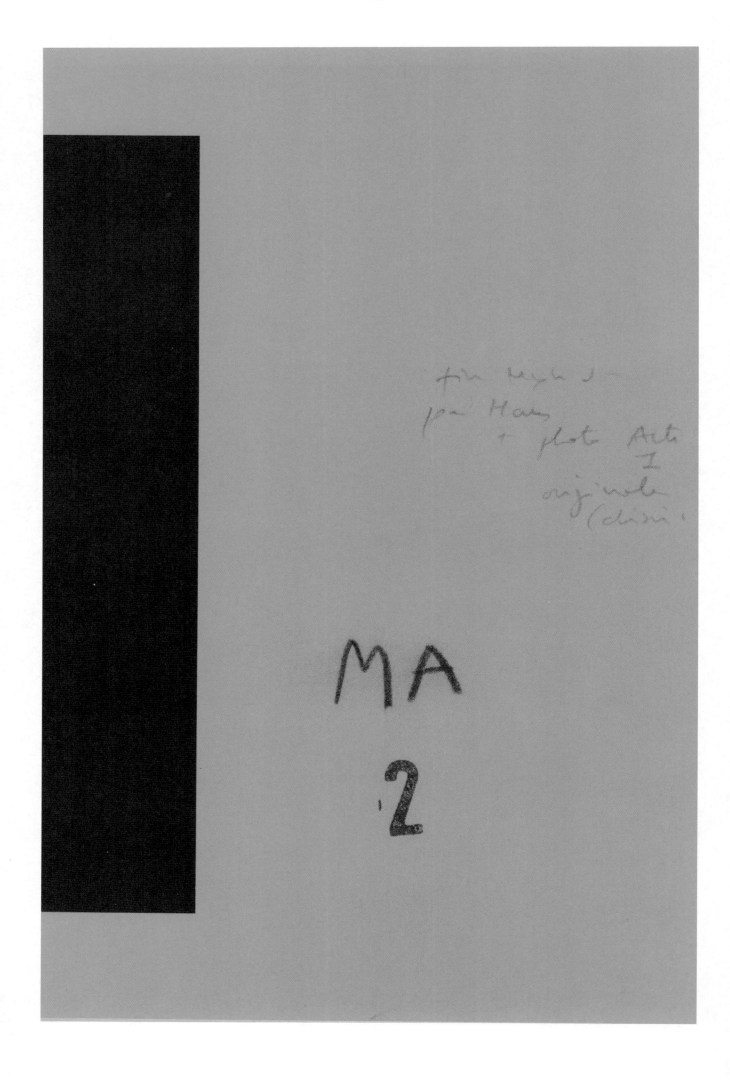

M A est le pré-projet de la nouvelle création
de la Compagnie Pierre Droulers.

MA is all of the following: a slit, a distance, a crack,
a difference, a split, a disposition, a boundary,
a pause, a dispersion, a blank, a vacuuum.
One can say that its function is infinitely close to Derrida's
espacement = becoming space.

Arata Isozaki, "A Fragmentary Portrait of Anyone" .

Les images de ce dossier sont issues de" S, M, L, XL" de Rem Koolhaas
et Bruce Mau.

MA

Bruxelles, mai 1999.

2002: Creation of *Sames*

SAMES

Choreography: Pierre Droulers

With: Stefan Dreher, Pierre Droulers

Lighting and set design: Ludovic Pré, Bertrand Lissoir

Video: Ludovic Pré

Assistant: Aurélien Desclozeaux

Costumes: Yohji Yamamoto

First performance: 6 February 2002, Friche La Belle de Mai, Marseille

Co-production: Charleroi/Danses

le milieu
de la
vie

MA
9

ma

James Joyce

As referenced in the work *Sames*, a contraction of 'James' and 'Samuel'.

Samuel Beckett   For one of them, rejoicing in the world as a whole; while, for the other one, almost nothing is even better.

Stefan Dreher and Pierre Droulers

Robert and Pierre Droulers

DAYS OF THE WEEK

In a large room, situated at the heart of a dance centre in Brussels, thirty tables put together end to end make up a rectangular space in the middle. On the tables are hundreds of documents that recall twenty-eight choreographies: scores, commentaries, notes, sketches, photos, photocopied articles, books, invitations, posters. In the middle, sitting at a lone table, Pierre Droulers and a few colleagues are in the middle of a brainstorming session on the organisation of all this material for the publication of a proposed book.

I remember already having encountered this problem during previous editorial ventures. When we try to set out the life or work of an older artist by opting for a chronological order, we end up with an uneven book because the quality and nature of the photos are extremely variable. At the beginning, we have black and white photos or cheap snapshots; then we come across attractive prints of photos with marked contrasts, certainly the work of professional photographers; then we discover a few poor-quality images taken from videos, and even two colour photocopies; finally, the first digital photos with pale colours and poor clarity, followed by digital photos that seem too clean, before discovering digital photos deliberately distorted, etc. It's not so much the diversity that poses a problem, but rather the chronology that determines a linear progression, making the composition of a book difficult, even impossible. Certainly, reversing the chronology allows, in certain cases, beginning with the most recent images, so that the book takes on the appearance of an archaeological excavation, where we dig down layer by layer, discovering the most recent layer at the beginning.

Presented in this way, the problem still seems straightforward. But to that is added the diversity of types of image for each work. Sometimes most of the images were taken during rehearsals, sometimes only during the performance, even sometimes after the performance. Occasionally there is a group photo; generally, there isn't one. Sometimes there are portraits of dancers, and sometimes not. In this one they were photographed in their final costumes; in that one in their everyday dancewear. In certain cases, the staging and the lighting were not yet ready. In a few snapshots, the photographer has succeeded in capturing an atmosphere, a lighting effect, a movement, a composition, but in most of them there is none of this. And we could go on, not to mention all the types of writing. Here, we've kept an interview, there, a review in English. There again, we've found a work transcript, or even a letter addressed to the mayor. Sometimes we come across a few dance commentaries and some sketches. Sometimes, nothing has survived.

To be honest, almost everything has disappeared: the general prevailing
mood at the time, the social or political significance of a particular venue,
the reputation of a dancer or a dramatist, the connotations of certain
costumes, the movement of the dancers, the arrangements, the lighting,
the music, the sound, the silence, the expectations and the reactions
of the audience, the rivalries between colleagues, the love affairs, the
friendships, the resentments and the joyfulness.

The picture that needs to be pinpointed goes off in three or five and even
seven directions, and in each of these directions, this picture spreads
outwards again and again like a firework going off. Because it's not a
question of dealing with a single artist here, but a group of artists –
in constant evolution – each of whom brings their personality and their
approach and who, through their coming together, create a new specific form.

It's not only Proust or Joyce who would be capable of rising to this
challenge, we then say to ourselves. And it's then that we remember that, for
Droulers, the universal and proteic approach of Joyce was inseparably linked
to the pared-down approach of Beckett. Those who watch his choreographies
see that he dreams of an intermediate form: a composition made up of a few
brushstrokes and light touches, pared down, but in counterpoint, capable
of conjuring up the whole universe. Each time, he begins with innumerable
discussions, images, texts, sounds, and suggestions from the dancers or
other collaborators, which he slowly puts together, like the pieces of a
puzzle, most of the material finally being rejected. The final composition
speaks to us about the world like a song or a painting, sometimes giving
us the impression that everything has been said because everything seems to
be there: the rain and the wind, the silence and the noise, love and death,
waiting and forgetting, the wheelbarrow and the shadow, the rustling tree
and the buzzing insect, the decisive word and the hesitant gesture.

We still find ourselves around the table in the space in the middle of
the assembled tables. I suggest organising the twenty-eight performances
alphabetically by title, and to present them in this order in the book.
That could end up producing both a varied and balanced publication. The end
of the book would also feature a chronological list of the performances, so
that one could also read the book in that order.

Pierre Droulers sets out another proposition. With his right hand, he
makes a shape of a small animal's head in order to give more weight to
his words. Half of what he says seems to be spoken by this hand, which
contributes to the thought process through very carefully chosen words:
'I would like to organise the book by the days of the week,' he says:

'Monday: preparation. Tuesday: action. Wednesday: communication. Thursday: expansion. Friday: feeling. Saturday: sedimentation. Sunday: being, not doing.' I was enchanted by this attractive definition of the days of the week, which immediately reminded me of a painter who told me that he represented each day of the week differently and that he would like, when the occasion arose, to paint them.

Then, Droulers showed me a *circular diagram* that he had put together himself.

Monday: mystery, shadow-light, duality, birth-death
Tuesday: epic, combat, small-big space, 'ugly is beautiful', daydream
Wednesday: reality-activity, men-women, game, gather
Thursday: The Fault, *felix culpa*, mechanism-machine, karma, infernal machine, abracadabra, the dreamed of peace, the farm
Friday: the hips, lyrical, moaning, dancing, kissing-hold back, Mary Magdalene, throwing balls, Judas kiss, forbidden, sex, fall, eclipse, loss, 'the coupling was not expected'
Saturday: individual, loss, waiting, isolation, *tenebrae*, the pain of bereavement, the path in the woods, heartbreak, war
Sunday: communion, redemption (mystical), Peace, shining white, good news, 'we are only drops', the void is inexistence, *fiat lux*

He also showed me a hand-drawn diagram by László Moholy-Nagy, *Plan of Finnegans Wake*, which had inspired his own diagram. Looking at it closer, apart from the circular shape, there was no similarity between the two diagrams. But I think I know why this work by Moholy-Nagy speaks to Droulers. *Finnegans Wake* is thought of by many people to be an inaccessible book. It is, in effect one of these polymorphic literary works that attempts to capture or reflect the complexity of the world through a complicated form. Yet, Moholy-Nagy's diagram briefly gives us the impression that he knew how to decipher the novel. Put another way, it embodies our dream to be able to understand everything and to elucidate everything.

However, each time that we have the impression of being able to organise reality - for example, by dividing it between day and night - we forget that we quite simply rediscover the words that we already used previously to describe it. We discover that we can name something day and night, and we are happy. But what about dusk? Moonlight? Animals that come alive at night? Underground animal and vegetable life? The eternal darkness of the universe, which only lights up when something catches fire or when invisible rays of light strike an object?

First of all, there was the shapeless darkness and then came the Word, which brought light. Or is it the reverse: did the realisation of our mortality come only after we had received the gift of language?

If we now go back to Droulers' diagram, we see that it's in fact an excellent design for a dance performance. It's presented like a three-dimensional fresco that changes with the passing of time. Thanks to the circular shape, several velocities are possible. At the front left of the stage, a week can last two minutes; at the back right-hand side, we see only the fragments of a Monday that slowly swings into action. And from the back left-hand side to the front right, Wednesday unfolds in a slow diagonal that lasts for the whole of the performance. The light and shadow can shine like a stroboscope, one melting into the other with an imperceptible slowness or dissolving into an indescribable fog.

On the advice of Ida de Vos and Ann Veronica Janssens, in 1996 I attended a dance performance by Pierre Droulers for the first time: *De l'air et du vent*. Back home I wrote a letter to the choreographer to thank him. I saw some things for the very first time. For the first time, in effect, I saw light on stage. Just like, years previously, I saw for the first time, in an Ingmar Bergman film, almost tangible shades of grey, in a scene that takes place in a church flooded by sunlight. I had the impression of seeing an almost tangible light, which lingered above the scene like an almost invisible bank of fog. I also saw a sublime leap by Stefan Dreher, which seemed to contain in mid-flight a very brief countermovement, which was apparently similar to certain hand movements of Thelonious Monk. The performance evolved through a series of lines, points, marks, plans, diagonals, horizontals and verticals: becoming a three-dimensional picture, appearing and disappearing at the same time. Suddenly I felt what dance could be: to draw, paint, write, think, watch, forget, hesitate, decide, act, rest. And all that in a four-dimensional space.

The other day I attended a performance of *MA*, sitting next to the most important collector of conceptual art in the country. At the end of the show the man said that he had found the performance sublime. He had found in it the beauty of his own collection, refined, pared down, almost disembodied. Joyce becoming Beckett.

We are still sitting at the table in the centre of this large dance studio. Droulers shows in broad outline what the book could look like if it were organised by days of the week. I realise that we are in the middle of a performance. The arrangement of the tables, the documents spread out, our gestures: everything is part of a new choreography, from which the book would be the result. I remember a Luis Buñuel film in which the protagonists suddenly realise that they are actors on a stage and do not know their lines. I think of Gustave Flaubert's long years of preparation and of whom it is said that he cut down a whole forest to make a toothpick. I think of the monk who sculpted ten thousand Buddhas, whose final ones – small sticks showing three nicks – could be held in one hand. This is how you make things, I say to myself, just like God created our world: briefly rummaging through a basket of small dried fruit, attacked by seventeen tiny flies, shaking it all up in the palms of his cupped hands, and finally sowing it all in the void, like throwing beautifully perfumed and coloured dice. From a distance, it all seemed very clear: a bit of earth and water, a drifting mist that lit up in blue a carpet of green moss, and tiny little things that moved, lit up for a short while before immediately disappearing. A layer of glistening foam that softly popped, almost inaudible, and which produced, even if briefly, *the Iliad*, and some pretty little tunes, and some rhythms that entice one to dream.

Montagne de Miel, 2 August 2016

Chögyam Trungpa   Meditation – and wearing similar glasses – is common to both of them.

le plafond

la porte

lu

99 possibilities

for only one

movement

MA production Ⓐ

23. 03. 00

mative

le recommencement

l'espace proche

t

la

le mot

Pour finir, elles ne quitteront plus leur chambre, arche de Noé,
forteresse intérieure; y rassemblant tout ce qui a pu occuper leur vie.
Les objets, livres, images, sont accumulés dans un désordre saisissant,
comme si tout leur passé devait être à portée de leur main, de leurs
yeux. L'oeil pourtant ne s'attarde pas sur les choses, pas plus qu'il
ne lit réellement. Il reste entre deux, glissant de motifs en motifs.
La juxtaposition, la superposition des éléments visuels crée un tissu, sorte
de tapis sans motif central, sans logique de symétrie ou de répétition.
Effet kaléidoscopique produisant un sentiment hypnotique. Rester dans
l'entre-deux, dans le vide de la vision. Et lorsqu'on dit des personnes âgées
qu'elles retombent en enfance, c'est du fait de leur capacité à s'abstraire,
à plonger dans un état picnoleptique. Ni nostalgie, ni crainte de l'avenir,
les motifs autobiographiques ne sont là que comme des miroirs qui ne
reflètent que la lumière et le vide[…]

Georges Didi Huberman in *La Demeure, la souche. Apparentements de l'Artiste*,
quoting Pascal Convert in *Le motif autobiographique*, Éditions de Minuit,
Paris, 1999.

2004:   Creation of *Inouï*
2008:   *Light No Light*, documentary film by Ludovica Riccardi about
         the creation of *Inouï*

INOUï
Choreography: Pierre Droulers
With: Olivier Balzarini, Sébastien Chatellier, Suni Löschner, Saori Miyazawa, Marielle Morales, Michel Yang,
Arnaud Meuleman
Artistic direction, assistant: Arnaud Meuleman
Soundtrack: Thomas Turine
Music: Beth Gibbons
Lighting: Jim Clayburgh
Set design: Pierre Droulers, Arnaud Meuleman
Collaboration: Ann Veronica Janssens, Michel François
First performance: 23 March 2004, Blac, Biennale Charleroi/Danses, Brussels
Co-production: Charleroi/Danses, Festival de Marseille, Festival d'Automne, Théâtre de la Ville. Aided by Centre
de Développement Chorégraphique Toulouse/Midi Pyrénées as part of the projet In Vivo. Supported by Théâtre de la
Balsamine, Centre Chorégraphique Nationale de Rennes et de Bretagne, l'Agence Wallonie-Bruxelles. In collaboration
with Bird

appartemen

1. Vestiair

- vêtements
- tablette
- clés
- courrier
- waiting room
- changement

un nouvel espace à créer "Le Black"
appartement — apparentement
les fonctions du corps — les emotions
l'entrée ⟶ positionnement
la cuisine ⟶ manger, partager
la chambre ⟶ intimité
le salon ⟶ recreation communication
la salle de bains ⟶ le corps en parties
la cave ⟶ l'inconscient
le grenier ⟶ la memoire ecrite.

2. Couloir

- vas et viens
- passages
- étroit, vide
- pas d'accroc
- lieu écho tiqu
- « être déjà da

3. Cuisi

- « contrôle
- chaud
- lieu de tra
- sons/bruit

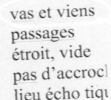

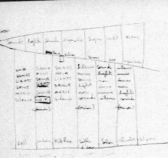

Light no Light

**INOUI
2004**

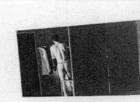

6. Cham

construit a
intimité
lâcher pri
imaginati

lon

5. Salle

eu d
alité

unicolore
vapeur - b
ablution
rituel

7. Cagibi :

sombre
petit
fermé
complexe
riche
lieu d'incons
pas de temps

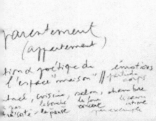

parentement
(appartement)

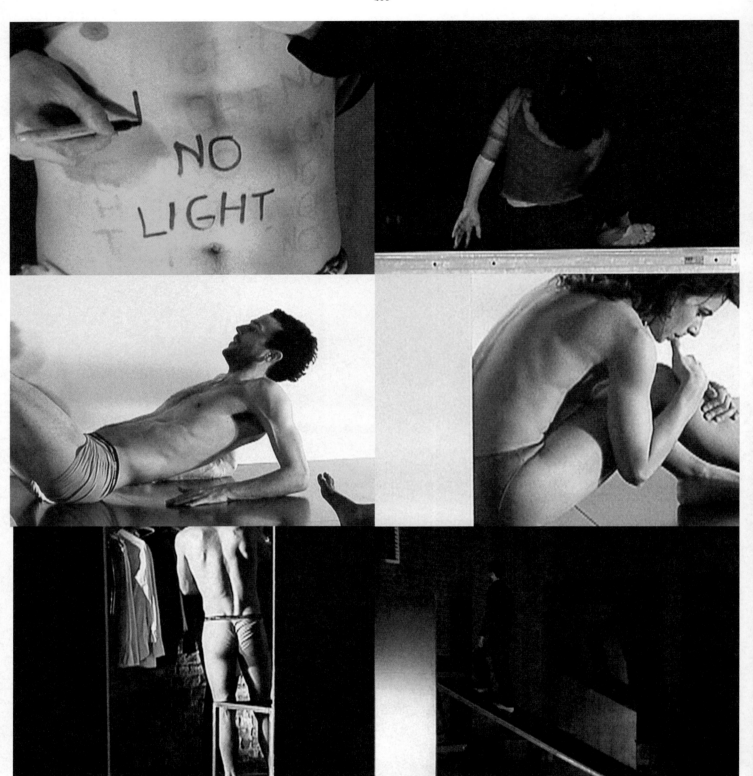

2000: Creation of *MA-I* by Ann Veronica Janssens
2001–04: Creation of Bird, dance studio at Cap 15, Marseille
2003: Ann Veronica Janssens' exhibition *8'26''* in Marseille, with Laure Prouvost and Bram Droulers
2003: *Carte Blanche* at Théâtre de la Balsamine, Brussels, and creation of *Parades*
2003–04: Creation of *Suspension temporelle*
2004: Training course and meeting with the Centre Chorégraphique Nationale de Rennes/Bretagne and the École des Beaux-Arts de Rennes
2005: Participation in the project *Agora* by Simon Siegmann
2006: Participation in the project *La Ricarda* of Michel François
2006: Two-handed project with Michel François

MA-I
Installation project and concept: Ann Veronica Janssens, Pierre Droulers
Realisation: Ann Veronica Janssens, Jim Clayburgh
First performance: 19 May 2000, Le Chorégraphique, Tours

SUSPENSION TEMPORELLE
Choreography: Pierre Droulers, in response to an invitation by Ann Veronica Janssens
With: Mathias Poisson, Eric Houzelot
Artistic direction, assistant: Arnaud Meuleman
First performance: 7 November 2003, Musée d'art contemporain, Marseille
Co-production: Marseille Objectif Danse

PARADES
Choreography and set design: Pierre Droulers
With: Stefan Dreher, Celia Hope Simpson, Katrien Vandergooten, Michel Yang/I-Fang Lin, Harold Henning
Music: Mathieu Boogaerts, Troublemakers, Émilie Simon
First performance: 5 June 2003, Festival Danse à la Balsa (Carte Blanche to Pierre Droulers), Brussels

AGORA
Installation project and concept: Simon Siegmann
Choreography: Pierre Droulers
Text: Jean-Michel Espitallier
Music: George van Dam
Musicians: Angélique Wilquie, Jan Kuiken, Géry Cambier, Tom Pauwels
Dancers: Shila Anaraki, Olivier Balzarini, Amit Hadari, Naîma Fahim Lamarti, Harold Henning, Sofie Kokaj, Arnaud Meuleman, Vincent Minne, Saori Miyazawa, Katrien Vandergooten, Marielle Morales, Ludovic Pré, Yuki Sakai, Uiko Watanabe, Michel Yang
Production: Margarita Production
Co-production: Charleroi/Danses, Kunstenfestivaldesarts

CHAPTER THREE

CONFLAGRATION

2007:   creation of *Flowers*
2008:   *Flowers (I see you)*, documentary film by Sima Khatami about
          the creation of *Flowers*

FLOWERS
Choreography: Pierre Droulers
With: Olivier Balzarini, Yoann Boyer, Sébastien Chatellier, Manon Greiner, Marielle Morales, Jara Serrano, Katrien
Vandergooten, Michel Yang, Arnaud Meuleman, Bruno Olivier
Artistic direction, assistant: Arnaud Meuleman
Soundtrack: Thomas Turine
Music: Steve Roden, Roxy Music, Public Image Ltd
Set design: Eric Chevalier, Yves Godin, Sima Khatami, Anne Masson, Arnaud Meuleman
Lighting: Yves Godin
Publication: Sofie Kokaj
First performance: 5 May 2007, La Raffinerie, Kunstenfestivaldesarts, Brussels
Production: Charleroi/Danses
Co-production: Kunstenfestivaldesarts. Aided by DANCE, supported by the European Union as part of Culture 2000

embras

habiter son ombre
habiter l'attente

BEIN

1 une residence dans un atelier à St. Remy
de l'Ile
2) une creation sur l'intime
le sexe, le desir,
l'oubli... la mort

renaissance.
Shanghai
éclat de brillance

Graphiste !

**FLOWERS
2007**

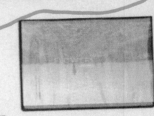

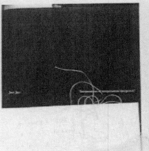

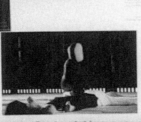

19 MAY 2016

It's 18 December 2006, my birthday, I am forty-four years old.
That day, me and my suitcase on wheels, super-noisy on the wet cobblestones
of Molenbeek, were heading towards La Raffinerie to meet the creative team
behind *Flowers*. I thought I was calmly arriving for a job that had begun a
few weeks earlier.

I hardly knew Pierre Droulers. I took the risk to work with him and
to accept his invitation after a single meeting two months previously,
following a show for which I did the lighting. He too took the same risk.
We spoke twice on the phone, he sent me a few videos, I loved the beginning
of *MA*, it's OK, let's give it a go. Despite the lack of exchanges, I tried
to be very responsive to the project, I had time to devote to it. I probably
didn't want to be ungenerous, I wanted to be in Brussels.

Pierre didn't want me involved at the beginning of the work at Saint-Rémy
in November, that suited me, I understood his wishes as much as his fears
about me being confronted by a group of dancers. He spoke to me about things
that were a bit obscure for me, chromotherapy, our interior colour… Me who,
in relation to lighting, tries to steer clear of all symbolism, psychology,
even abstraction, in order to maintain an essentially concrete approach.
Confronted with someone other than him, I would initially have reacted by
stepping back; I felt, despite everything, by listening to him, by looking
at the pictures of his shows, that our attitudes to time, space, plasticity,
choreographic material, scenography, light, sound or poetics, could connect
up together. I was curious to get to work and to explore with him the
enormous number of ideas hardly sketched out, but supported by deep active
thinking, nourished by experience. Pierre is older than I am but we share
a common knowledge, which creates affinities for certain artists, a sort of
familiarity. We spoke a bit (not too little, we always speak too much) about
houses, space being permanently transformed, giant origami, of the porosity
in each of our specific characters. I didn't know where I was going but I
went on anyway without preconceptions. I got more than I bargained for!

So, at eleven o'clock in the morning, straight from the Gare du Midi, me
and my suitcase went up to the fifth-floor creative studio, by the fastest
reacting lift in the world! I had hardly pushed the button and there I was,
with the door open! No time to ponder, so much the better.

Pierre: 'Ah, Yves, hi there. I'll finish the warm up with the dancers and
then we can sit at a table so that you can tell us a bit about what you
spoke about on the phone. OK with you?'

Me (frozen to the spot): 'Er, well yes, OK.'

Usually for me, if I can speak like this, the early days are a time of
observation, of making contact, above all with a team of people and a new

job. One hour later I was sitting at the table in front of Pierre, all the
dancers unknown to me, the stage managers, an assistant director, under
the watchful eye of Sima Khatami's camera, which was recording the entire
working procedure.

Thrown in at the deep end, no decompression chamber. After a few general
reflections from me, probably lacking conviction, Pierre suggested that
I use the time while the dancers were having lunch to prepare, with the
help of the technicians, a work session for the afternoon, around the idea
of manoeuvring tarpaulins that I had just mentioned. The tarpaulins were
bought on the spot.

I was unsettled, I didn't know if it was a sort of provocation or even
perversity to put me in this situation, but I rather see in it the desire to
want to immerse me in a physical and mental state that would necessitate a
connection with the intensity of the moment and create a link with the whole
team. It was surely a question of avoiding taking a backseat or a critical
position, which would then prevent direct action. Paradoxically, a feeling
of confidence grew in me – not self-confidence exactly, but rather the energy
of someone who has nothing to lose and everything to gain.

A first session was astonishingly productive and triggered other ideas:
we ordered 200 m² of cardboard sheets as well as rolls of the same
cardboard, so that we could experiment, in the form of an improvised stage
design workshop, with alterations of the stage that we could think of as
atmospheric. For four days, the stage area was permanently in action, with
the dancers as well as Pierre, myself and the technicians: the dance that
was created was one of space, the bodies one after the other invited, within
a precise framework, to create a collective composition.

When we talk about the stage, it's as much about the objects that inhabit
it, the bodies that live there, the sounds that pass over it or the lighting
that flows through it. A body will be sound, light, a dancing light, a sound
solid as stone, a stone soft like a sponge, a gust of wind like a guitar riff.
The floor will become the ceiling, the sky will become a wall, a fissured
desert a deconstructed sea, a light box a blooming flower, a reel of thread a
river of blood.

In this way, we created enough material for ten performances, we kept
enough to make five, in order in the end to make just one. We worked on
different scales of space and time, on the stage, in the workshop, where
rubbing shoulders together were drawings, texts, images, models, books;
those for the daytime, which were focused, and those for the night-time,
which went on forever.

To jump in the deep end, to break down the barriers between the artistic

performers and creators, at least at this stage of the work, to nurture a
wild and jubilant energy for those who like to blur the conventional lines
of their medium. Pierre was not conventional, and I loved being on stage and
sharing together the 'making' with him.

  There are images that linger, explicit phrases ('I will kill those in
doubt!')… Pierre, with a gentle brutality, was the master of ceremonies for
harmonious chaos. With him, very carefully protected, there was an energy
that we described as punk, that emphasised urgency, improvisation, chaos,
irreverence, counterbalanced or fed by a different relationship to time,
vision, thought, which came from eastern influences. The result is that
we will never be fixed in a picture album, but always walking a tightrope
between a youthful wildness and the wisdom of those who take the time
to watch and listen. This tension is even the driving force of the work,
the bodies, the dance, the light and the sound, permeated by explosive
intensity as much as silence; each second deeply linked to the distortions
of our inner self. For a long time, it was difficult to sign up to what we
all called 'dance', probably because from the outset dance was everywhere,
in the precise elegant movement of two technicians turning the dance mat
over - the stage going from white to black in record time - in a tarpaulin,

a huge bed for insomniac children, in the twisting of a body or the
spiderlike walk of another.

We built our home over the course of five months, and this home was
baroque, poetic, sensual, violent, excessive, chaotic and tender. There was
also the discipline of composition, a precise and complex orchestration of
miscellaneous elements in the service of an extremely lively ambiguity.
It wasn't so much about mixing up art and life, we were the life. We were
living it and afterwards it lived in us.

Flowers is one of those creations that remains with one. It's there,
the production process that guided it now always influences my work, it
underlined the pleasure of creating links between different disciplines, to
look for connections, or to make a lot out of very little. An immersion in a
large invigorating and reinvigorating bath.

Looking back, I am convinced that we had the rare privilege of having the
means to create coherence, coherence between our desires and the elements
of time, space, material and human, to really be there in the exploration
of stage-writing. Our work should be regularly fed by such processes, where
time, space, human and financial resources react in real time with the needs
of our experience, and are not a luxury but an integral part of the act of
creation.

At the beginning of *Flowers* is a magnificent opening scene, a
concentration of bodies, symbolic violence, physical tension: Pierre, front
of stage, loads a rifle, stands firm, settles and fires towards a stick of
chalk lodged in the far wall, a precise gesture, minimal, the sound tears
open the space, which then opens up: electric. Curtain…

MANON GREINER   FLOWERS

I felt fragile and indestructible at
the same time - like life, which dies
and grows everywhere.

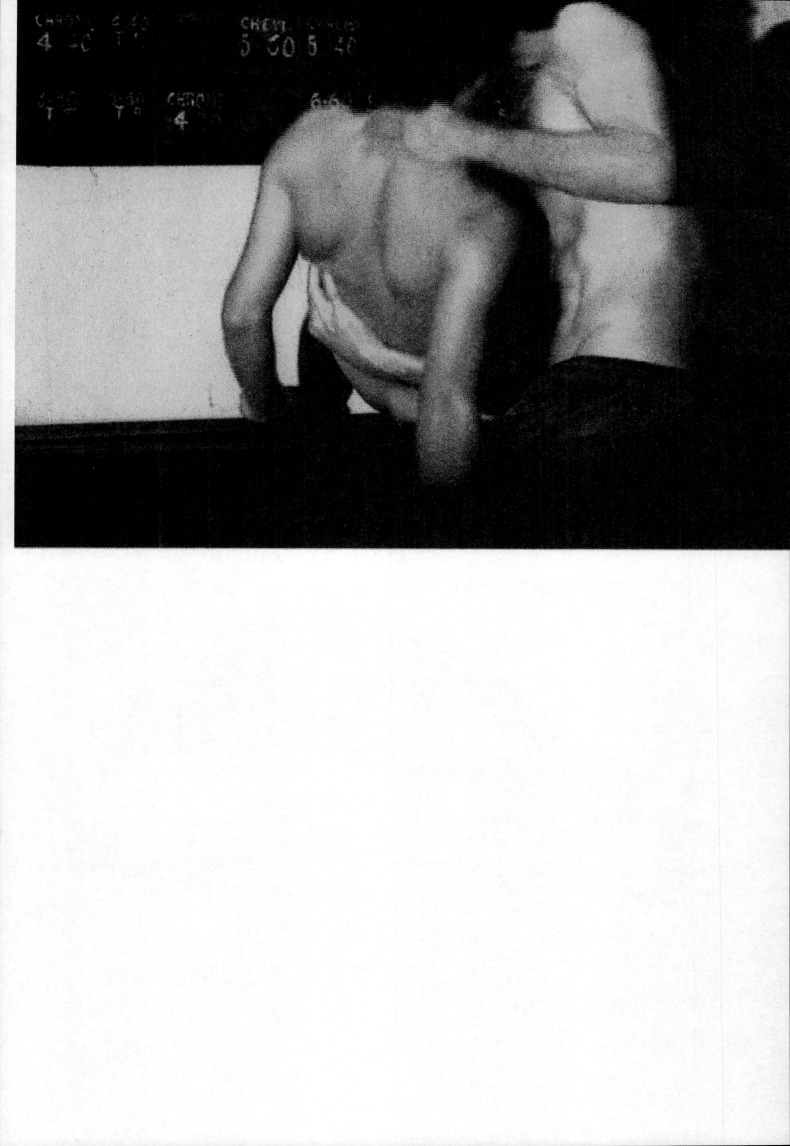

2007:   Creation of *All in All*
2009:   Performance of *Two Night Ping-Pong*

ALL IN ALL
Choreography: Pierre Droulers
With: Fernando Carrión Caballero, Maïté Cebrian Abad, Louis-Clément da Costa,
Peggy Grelat-Dupont, Yang Jiang, Caelyn Knight, Franck Laizet, Jérôme Piatka
Choreography, assistant: Marielle Morales
Music: eRikm
Set design: Pierre Droulers, Simon Siegmann
Lighting: Simon Siegmann
Costumes: Own
First performance: 19 June 2007, Théâtre National Populaire, Lyon
Production: Opéra de Lyon as part of the 'Osez La Danse d'Aujourd'hui' project

TWO NIGHT PING-PONG
Carte blanche 'Welcome to my world' and 'Standpunkte', Schwere Reiter (Tanz/Theater/Musik)
Choreography: Pierre Droulers
With: Olivier Balzarini, Stefan Dreher
Assistant: Anna Konjetzky
First performance: 9 October 2009, Munich
Production: Tanztendenz München
Co-production: Charleroi/Danses. Supported by Kulturreferat, Landeshauptstadt München

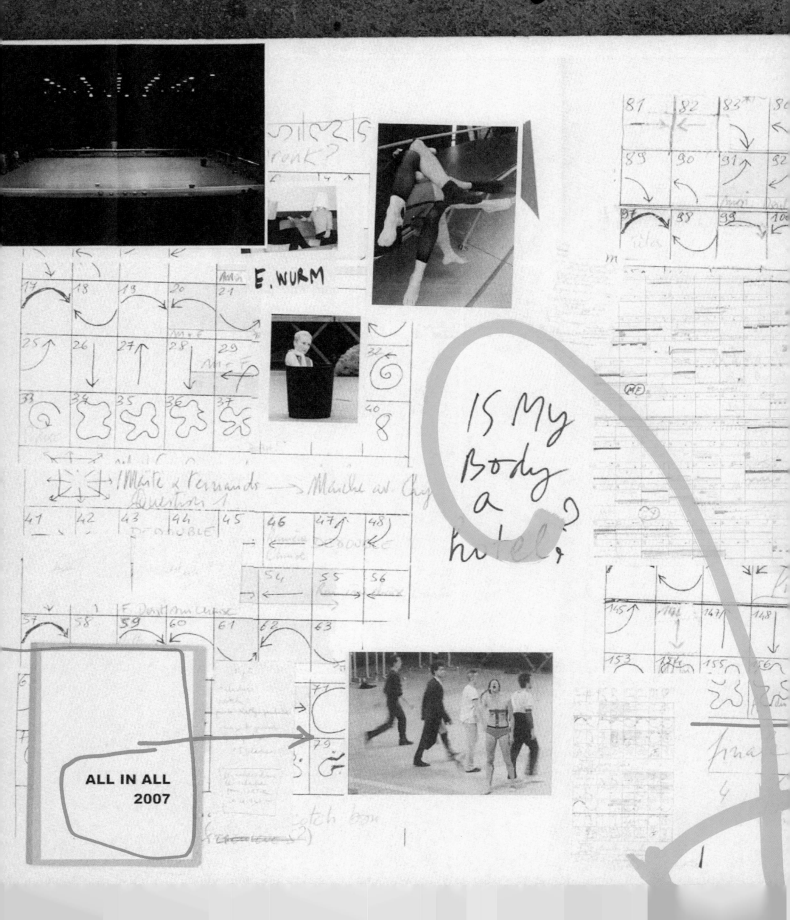

E. WURM

IS My
Body
a
hotel?

ALL IN ALL
2007

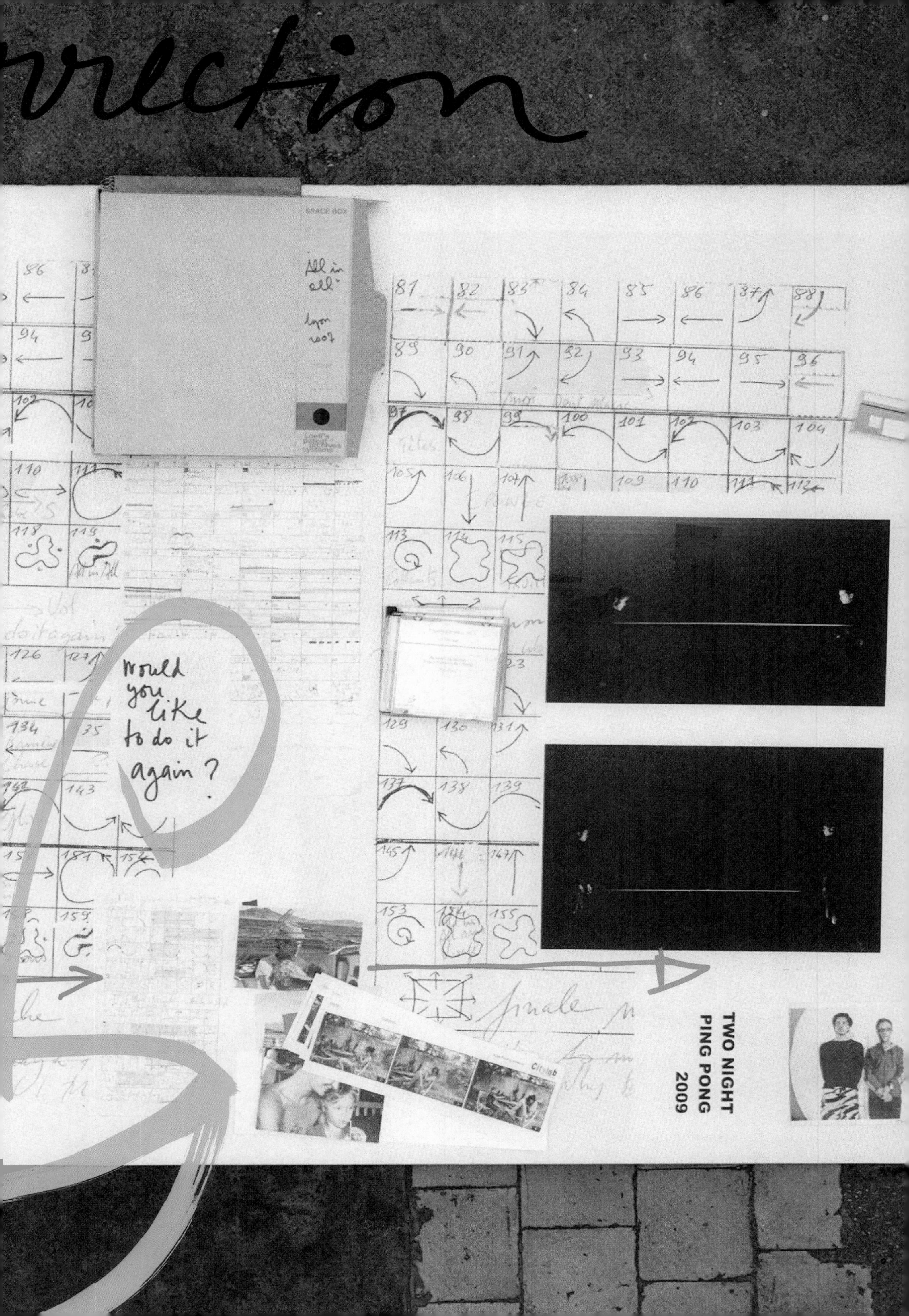

rection
would you like to do it again?
TWO NIGHT
PING PONG
2009

IS MY
Body
a
hotel?

would you like to do it again?

2009:   Creation of *Walk Talk Chalk*

WALK TALK CHALK
Choreography: Pierre Droulers
With: Hanna Ahti, Stefan Dreher, Clémence Galliard, Thomas Hauert, Martin Roehrich, Olivier Balzarini, Nixon Fernandès
Music and video: Denis Mariotte
Artistic direction, assistant: Olivier Balzarini
Drama advisor: Antoine Pickels
Lighting: Yves Godin
Artistic collaboration: Michel François, Gwendoline Robin
Costumes: d'andt
First performance: 6 May 2009, Kaaitheater, Kunstenfestivaldesarts, Brussels
Production: Charleroi/Danses
Co-production: Kunstenfestivaldesarts, Festival de Marseille, Théâtre Le Merlan, Marseille, Marseille Objectif Danse, La Bâtie - Festival de Genève, Théâtre du Grütli, Geneva. Supported by Les Brigittines, Centre national de danse contemporaine d'Angers. Aided by Wallonie-Bruxelles Internationale and Wallonie-Bruxelles Théâtre/Danse

WTC
montée s
chute p
chute f
devants s
realité

WALK TALK
CHALK
2009

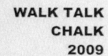

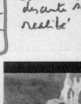

chute de la passion   chute de la
chute de l'esseulé   chute du
chute de l'assassin   chu

eux encore

PARTITION
DENIS

DÉVORANT
LE CIEL

ux pa

hs

SUICIDE
SÛTRA

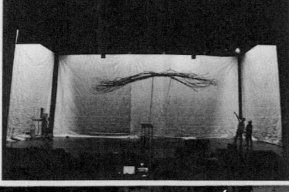

chute de l'intimité
chute de l'argent
la Beauté   chute du héros
chute de la représenta

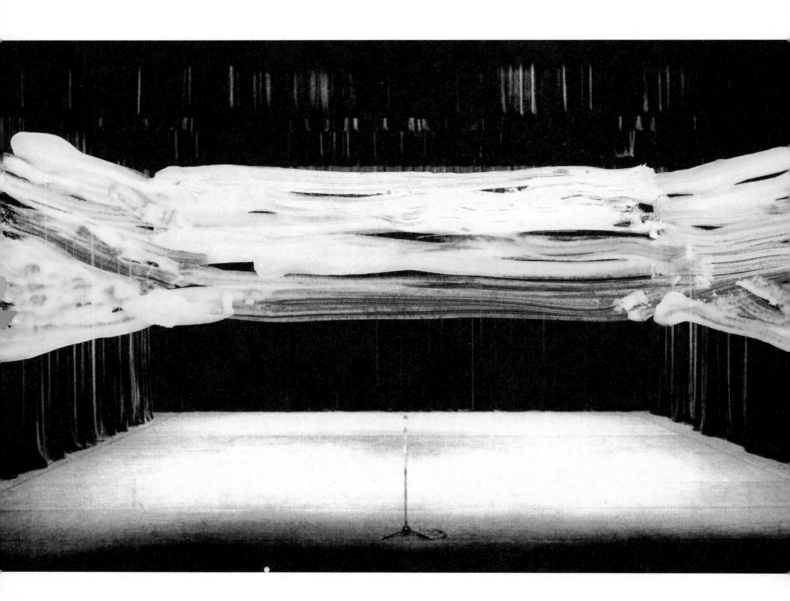

DENIS   MARIOTTE

26 MARCH 2011

_____

During the creation of the work *Walk Talk Chalk*, I remember often having had
this quotation by Spinoza in my head:
  'I understand reality and perception to be one and the same thing.'
  Sometimes, in the middle of working, I said it out loud in front of
Pierre, who made me repeat it, to draw out the resonance. Most of the time
that triggered a smile that encompassed many things.

LETTRES
de la
Religieuse
Portugaise

Hölderlin

Mit gelben Birnen hänget
Und voll mit wilden Rosen
Das Land in den See,
Ihr holden Schwäne,
Und trunken von Küssen
Tunkt ihr das Haupt
Ins heilignüchterne Wasser.

Weh mir, wo nehm ich, wenn
Es Winter ist, die Blumen, und wo
Den Sonnenschein,
Und Schatten der Erde ?
Die Mauern stehn
Sprachlos und kalt, im Winde
Klirren die Fahnen.

Moitié de la vie
De poires jaunes
Et de rosiers sauvages toute chargée
La terre est en suspens au-dessus du lac,
Ô cygnes gracieux,
Enivrés de baisers,
Vous plongez la tête
Dans la sainte sobriété de l'eau.

Ô douleur, où trouverai-je,
À l'hiver, les fleurs et où
La lumière du soleil
Et les ombres de la terre ?
Les murs se dressent
Froids et muets, dans le vent
Tintent les drapeaux.

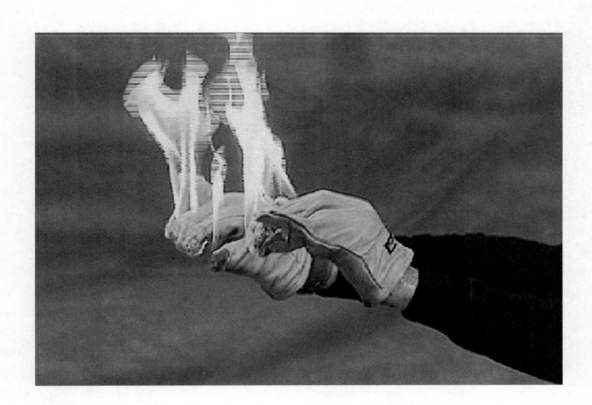

2012: Travel in Japan with Olivier Balzarini, Arnaud Meuleman, Yuji Oshima, Caroline Vermeulen, Yuko Hirai, Bram Droulers and meeting with Shiro Takatani.

KYOTO
EXPERIMENT
2012

潤一郎

LE NUE

un film de KANETO SHINDO
musique de HIKARU HAYASHI

tu
n'as rien
vu ....

Ishima   Naoshima

2013:   Creation of *Soleils*

SOLEILS
Choreography: Pierre Droulers
With: Louis Combeaud/Yoann Boyer, Malika Djardi, Stanislav Dobák, Youness Khoukhou,
Renan Martins de Oliveira/Louis-Clément da Costa, Benjamin Pohlig, Peter Savel, Jonathan Schatz, Katrien Vandergooten
Artistic direction, assistant: Arnaud Meuleman
Soundtrack: Beth Gibbons, Eric Thielemans
Set design: Chevalier-Masson
Collaboration: Yuji Oshima
Lighting: Pierre Droulers, Marc Lhommel
Costumes: Jean-Paul Lespagnard
First performance: 9 May 2013, La Raffinerie, Kunstenfestivaldesarts, Brussels
Production: Charleroi Danses
Co-production: Kunstenfestivaldesarts, Festival de Marseille, Maison de la Culture de Tournai/Next Festival

There's a certain slant of light,
On winter afternoons,
That oppresses, like the weight
Of cathedral tunes.

Heavenly hurt it gives us;
We can find no scar,
But internal difference
Where the meanings are.

None may teach it anything,
'Tis the seal, despair,An imperial affliction
Sent us of the air

When it comes, the landscape listens,
Shadows hold their breath;
When it goes, 'tis like the distance
On the look of death

EMILY DICKINSON

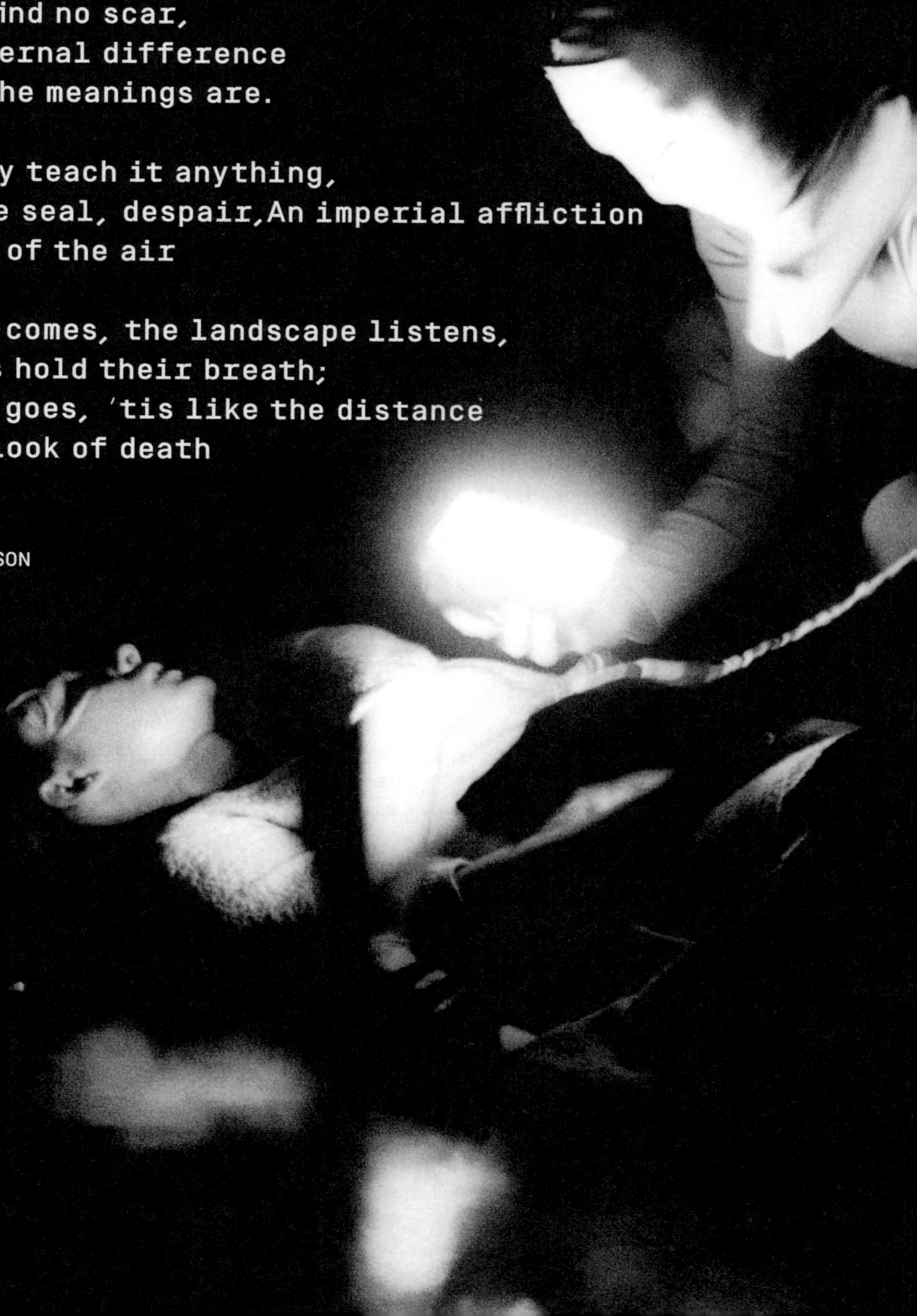

Do not go gentle into that good night,
Old age should burn and rave at close of day;
Rage, rage against the dying of the light.

Though wise men at their end know dark is right,
Because their words had forked no lightning they
Do not go gentle into that good night.

Good men, the last wave by, crying how bright
Their frail deeds might have danced in a green bay,
Rage, rage against the dying of the light.

Wild men who caught and sang the sun in flight,
And learn, too late, they grieved it on its way,
Do not go gentle into that good night.

Grave men, near death, who see with blinding sight
Blind eyes could blaze like meteors and be gay,
Rage, rage against the dying of the light.

And you, my father, there on the sad height,
Curse, bless, me now with your fierce tears, I pray.
Do not go gentle into that good night.
Rage, rage against the dying of the light.

DYLAN THOMAS

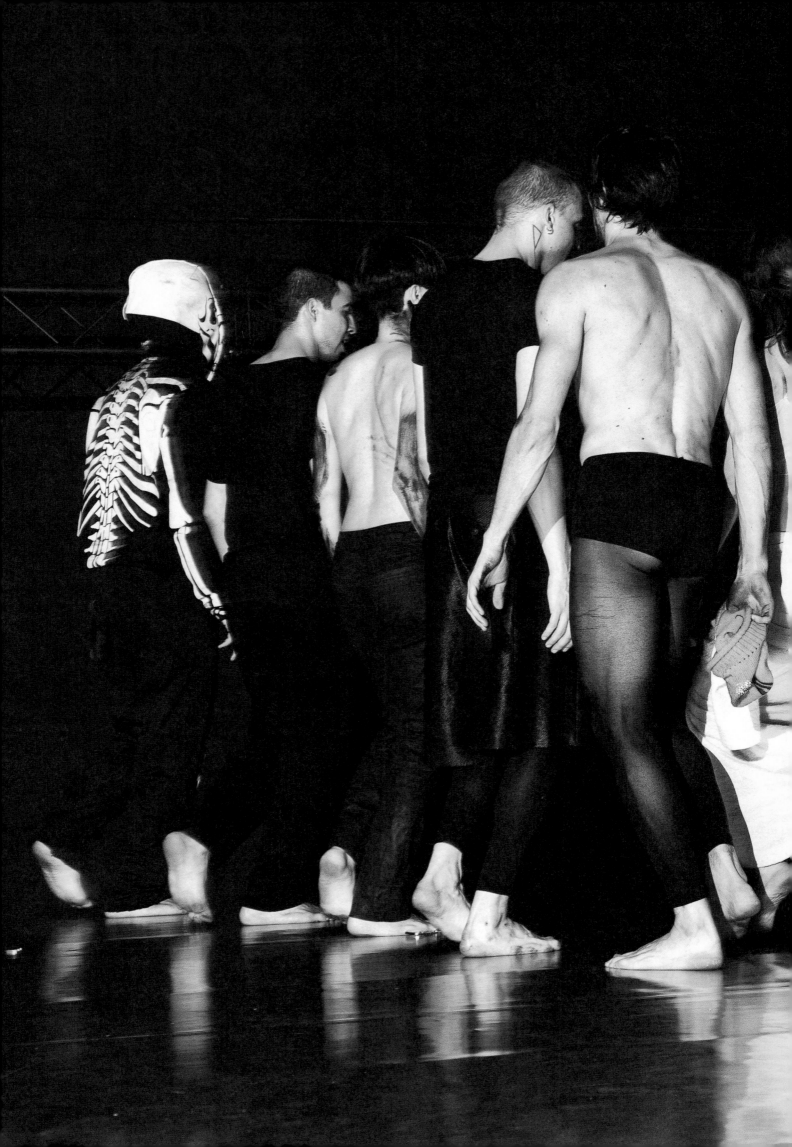

2013–16:   Creation and development of the *Danseur* programme
2014:   Creation of *Each Today is Yesterday's Tomorrow*
2016:   Creation of *Bird in a zoo*

EACH TODAY IS YESTERDAY'S TOMORROW
Choreography: Youness Khoukhou, Pierre Droulers
With: Youness Khoukhou
Music: Moondog, 'Each Today is Yesterday's Tomorrow'; Janis Joplin with Big Brother and the Holding Company,
'All is Loneliness'
First performance: 20 April 2016, La Raffinerie, Brussels
Production: Charleroi Danses

BIRD IN A ZOO
Choreography: Stefan Dreher, Pierre Droulers, Wagner Schwartz
With: Stefan Dreher, Wagner Schwartz
First performance: 13 October 2016, La Raffinerie, Brussels, as part of the *Danseur* festival
Production: Charleroi Danses

MALIKA   DJARDI

26 OCTOBER 2016

_____

Pierre Droulers was holding auditions for *Soleils* at La Raffinerie.
   It was the last day of auditions and I began to enjoy myself, to release
the tension. Pierre had set us a quite spirited dance move, both rigorous
and nonchalant at the same time. It was my turn to go: to feel scrutinised.
   But I felt good there and I danced, and looking up I saw Pierre watching
me, and then he winked at me. At that moment, we perhaps chose each other.
He was sitting down but everything within him was dancing and laughing, we
mutually charged each other. This smile was the future, if it was dazzling
like a gemstone or calm like Buddha's. One generation watching another,
imitating, being nourished and communicating with intensity and volatility.
And we shared together the story of *Soleils*.

   Above all Pierre taught me to think with the body.
   During the conception of *Soleils* he adopted a superior attitude in
relation to most of us. An attitude almost like the haughtiness of a
domineering youth. Many of us hadn't worked with other choreographers before
this experience and despite that we were full of assurance. Great schools,
big egos.
   Pierre was very generous and in front of us sometimes appeared bereft
during the conception.

   "You need to retain a naivete": he underlined this need and necessity to
discard judgements and preconceptions for his work. To dispossess in order
to become possessed.
   Well no doubt naivete is relative: we all have aesthetic preferences,
a story, techniques. We learnt about somatics, sensitivity, efficiency,
concepts, distance and even non-dance. We devoured the history of dance.
   What does naivete mean in relation to the conception of a choreography,
when we are being inspired by texts, music, images, poems and films? To
try and forget how to dance and look for a movement that we've never done
before? Is it just an attitude? Maybe absorb all that and experience a
spontaneous natural reaction with your skin, your weight, the desire to
dance?
   We don't know. We must therefore look for it. We must always take on
the experience to keep dancing and innovating, in order to find this new
language.
   To throw yourself into it.
   I've certainly had few opportunities to relive these four months'
experience of work with Pierre Droulers on *Soleils*. Why? There's no more
money, we're told! And why? Economics is an aspect of our work and there

is less and less money. There's less and less work and more and more
millionaires. There are a lot of artists but often the same well-known
names. And we, the little people, we talk a bit but we are often quickly
stifled.

Not everybody can speak at the same time or want to express themselves.

To listen is also to cultivate, to share, to create space and then
sometimes to start laughing loudly at the masquerade.

Post – *Soleils*:
Sa prière, first project, solo documentary that put my approach to dance
and my mother's religion side by side. It seems that religions are only an
adaptation of sun worship.

Like Pierre, I like to continue to smile, to be naïve without being
a sucker (I don't really like cynics, a question of taste). The most
important thing for me is energy, like the sun's energy. The energy of an
unconditional freedom.

What interests me, is the way in which in which humankind continually
creates and shares information. I like to question myself on the
relationship between abstract and figurative. How languages are formed and
reinvented.

Like the body and the world, culture is transformed with the test of time.

Choreographic language must always reinvent itself to stay contemporary.
As soon as it becomes standardised, categorised, it loses its topicality.

The body of the performer is shaped by enigmas and by biology that is more
objective than fanciful. It is almost a physical object. It's on the body
that we project and it's the body that activates the choreographic language
that has been imparted to it. The performer is the material itself of this
transformation. Creation in dance is also a question of posterity.

Where do we come from and where are we going? But above all to what are we
susceptible?

To live from day to day. And dance day and night.

It's an absurd activity, dance: to impose nothing and yet to succeed in
destroying the certainties about the body, the style, the world; it speaks
without saying anything, it lives there, now, free, everywhere; contemporary
dance is anarchic!

A Spanish programme director who was putting on *Horion*, my second project,

for his festival, recently told me that he thought I was an anarchist (he doesn't know that I like luxury products a bit too much).

Unfortunately, "contemporary dance" is also a sort of luxury product: we are marinated in a *showbiz society*, gathered together in a communalist elitism, in artistic ghettos, specialists of our crafts that don't involve many other people than ourselves. Dance should perhaps get out of the theatre. Use other settings. Its already doing so. Dance in the street like "Nuit debout"? But where is "Nuit debout" now? So, dance in the street like my skate-boarding friends!

It's difficult to maintain desire and energy when money is short. Today life is so expensive. It's a hell of a trap!

We need more spaces that survive due to the involvement and engagement of everyone, where the network of political, economic and artistic responsibility is working, and where social diversity exists.

In New York, artistic communities get together and reinvent new systems based on the exchange of services. That makes me think in fact that I began dancing thanks to Maguy Marin, who ran the choreography centre at Rillieux-la-Pape, in the Lyon suburbs. She opened up her professional teaching to everyone, for free.

My "turfu" dance will be a science-fiction dance.

The production of signs, energies and images. Aren't we going to revolutionise that?

The body remains a body: being a spectator or a performer.

Maybe holograms of dancers will be invented, or applications for "dance performance", dance with enhanced reality. Will concepts and technology conquer the body, the flesh and its fragility? It remains to be proved.

Like a rolling stone, like the earth that turns.

Life on Mars?

Certain people say that we are descended from extra-terrestrials, others from monkeys or a type of reptile. Can we still evolve physically and still adapt to the environment?

We have already experienced periods of intellectual regression in the history of mankind, and the annihilation of the Mayas: nuclear war or natural catastrophe? It's sure that nothing will remain from the history of mankind, not even this book.

The earth or technology? The stock-exchange or life?

"We need to destroy all our systems" they say! Internet and virtual reality as counter balances, against information, too much information.

If we destroy the current order, will we be able to live at the level of our expectations, and to have the courage to take on the responsibility?

What do we keep if we want to change everything?

However, there are some good things: clean and warm studios, intermittence, the memory of Pierre who had bought his bottle of Chateau thingy during the composition of *Soleils*: that's what we want!

We liiiiiiiiiiiike it.

And it's goooooooooooood.

We are always saved by love and that won't change. Well….

11 MAY 2016

Talking about Pierre - it seems that I've already spoken about him... but
I can't find my notes. So much the better, I know what I wanted to say... but
we don't always want to say it. It will be better not to talk in the way
that we speak, don't you think? Pierre opened up a specific space for me in
Belgium - Belgium's a specific country... not that much. Pierre, it seems that
what I propose is to open up spaces that don't exactly resemble the way that
we speak - and even that there's no use speaking about life, the real thing
is so much bigger. It's this accompanying, this colour that I feel in his
work. Like speaking to a painter... We've worked together but we don't know
what we've done. We do know (maybe), but there's no point in talking about
it. 'Spontaneity is the secret of life,' said Federico Fellini. Friendship,
the term 'friendship' gets close to it. Pierre saw many of my shows, even
the most obscure. I think at the beginning, guided by the girls, Anisia,
Sofie. To this day, I've only seen one of his shows, a long time afterwards,
but it's the same (*De l'air et du vent*, in its rerun). At La Raffinerie,
invited by Pierre, I put on *Blektre* by Nathalie Quintane and Charles
Torris, a piece that Hubert Colas had asked me to 'create in space' and
that - through using an ingenious ploy: recording the voices of numerous
characters and of the stage directions by only two actors - I succeeded
in elevating to the rank of a 'major show'. The performers on stage acted
by miming to a pre-recorded soundtrack that wasn't synchronised, a sort of
don't-give-a-damn free-wheeling happening. The version put on in Brussels
was in the end more 'professional', more polished than it was when Pierre
saw it at the La Colline in Paris, more of an 'expansion of emptiness', with
more gaps, more aridity, and that he preferred. The following year there
was the great experience of *1ᵉʳ Avril* (thus called because it was the date
of the performance; and subtitled *Jour des fous*). Here, with a genuine, very
warm welcome from La Raffinerie, more money, one month in total I think, we
were able to put on two acts that I still find of an exquisite brilliance.
As the memories, the photos and the films bear witness. Tiny particles floated
in the air. I felt it was missing one act and in the run-up I hesitated;
with fifteen days or maybe only a week more, we could have done it. Pierre
encouraged me, the organisers gently restrained me in order to ensure that
the evening - the festival - did not go on too long, there was still a
concert on after us. I thought that the audience would only see, after all,
an incomplete work (two acts completely ready, and the space and the subject
matter conjuring up a third, the resolution). Of course, this third act was
never completed and it stuck in my mind: a sort of cosmic picnic bringing
together, in I don't know what intergalactic landscape, the protagonists
from the first and second acts (the two parts shown were very different, very

far apart). But, two years later a new *1er Avril* was put on in Paris, at the
Bouffes du Nord (on the same date of course), this time for ten performances.
It was based on the same premise as the first performance, very open, small
groups of music-hall performers and cinema actors lost in a floating,
flexible space-time. There was a lot to draw on from the first performance
in Brussels. The space here was too narrow, but Pierre was closely involved
in this sublime show, he accompanied me like a brother, he came to the
run-throughs and made comments, always spot on and useful, asking Lorenzo
De Angelis, for example, to double or triple the duration of his dances.
Pierre's son Bram was the star of the second part of the show, I don't know
how old he was, nine years old… I mention him here to underline again the
exceptional nature of this show. He was priceless, irresistible, incredibly
professional as well (to the point of disliking rehearsals because he only
wanted to perform in front of an audience), playing with Marlene Saldana
and Jean-Biche. Jeanne Balibar came back from Brazil with a samba costume
and songs that she translated from Caetano Veloso. Of course, it was at La
Raffinerie, for this show, that I met the sound engineer Benoît Pelé, who has
since always worked with me. As was my habit, we offered free previews, which
allowed us to act for a longer time and to finish putting the show together
along with the audience. It generated a real enthusiasm in Brussels. Lots
of people saw the show and didn't forget it. The following year, Pierre
didn't have the opportunity to put on this festival, *Compil d'Avril*, to
which he had invited me. So he created – with a smaller budget – a festival
of short performances called *Danseur*. And it was there that we put on, last
year, an acclaimed *Sacre du printemps*, a bit like when it was initially
created, when the critics called it *Massacre de printemps*: a sort of poetic
boxing match with two actors, Adrien Dantou and Gaël Sall, in a ring with
constantly changing light, naturally lively, with natural speed (that's to
say very fast, moving randomly) devised by Philippe Gladieux. Now that the
opportunities of openings with these spaces – which are as much Pierre's
as mine; I don't look to define them more precisely than that – and this
confidence diminishes, and the clouds are gathering, it seems to me, however,
that Pierre and I haven't finished working together at all, that in a sense
we still work together. As I said, friendship; in the end, all other words
last too long.

LUNE
SOLEIL
ECLIPSE
ETOILE
ETOILES
VENTS
MERS
VISAGES
PLAGES
MAGES

MARK TOMPKINS
Atelier Contact à Paris

FRANÇOIS VERRET
rencontre de Bagnolet

TABULA RASA

MICHEL FRANÇOIS
"Appartement à louer"
galerie de l'ERG/BXL

BÉNÉDICTE PESLE

"Le jour et la nuit"
de George BRAQUE

(Voyage LONDRE)

"Les illumination"
d'Arthur RIMBAUD

"Nouvelles et textes pour rien"
de Samuel BECKET

John CAGE

2-3 lignes de
CLAIRE DUVAL
· la jetée à Osten
· le bar "La Jetée" | à Cassis
· MARGUERITTE DU

Hubert Dombrecht

Hubert Dombrecht

Jean Luc BREUER

Hubert Dombrecht

groupe Triangle

groupe Triangle

ANNE FRÈRE

Anne FRÈRE

Pierre Droulers

Sheryl Sutton
Pierre Droulers

Kitty Kortes LYNCH
Pierre Droulers

Pascale MURTIN
François HIFFLER
Pierre Droulers

Caroline CAMUS
Didier Silhol
Pierre Droulers

Sheryl Sutton
Michèle Noiret
Patrick Beckers
Eric Sleichim
Pierre Droulers

STEVE LACY

Steve LACY
+ Steve POTTS

Ricardo Castro

Steve LACY
+ Steve POTTS

MINIMAL COMPACT

· Steve LACY
interprétation:
Steve SLEICHIM
· RICARDO CASTRO

Scénographie:
ROBERT DROULERS
+ Pierre Droulers

Complicité à
"DÉPAYSEMENT"
de Patrick BECKERS
(le Botanique/BXL)

Diapositives:
BRION GYSIN

groupe Triangle

Scénographie:
Philippe Mahillon

Scénographie:
Jean-Marie FIEVE

Raffinerie du
PLAN K
Bruxelles

· PARIS CLUB
· Festival du Marais
· Festival de la Rochelle

· Académie de Danse
de ROME
· Festival Klapstuk
à Louvain

· Festival d'EVREUX

· Beursschouwburg/BXL

· Festival d'EVREUX

Beursschouwburg/BXL

· Festival de
CHATEAUVALLON
· Raffinerie du
PLAN K/BXL

ART SERVIC

HEDGES	TAO	ALBA	TIPS	PIECES FOR NOTHING	LA JETÉE
1979	1980	1981	1982	1983	

407

Voyage JAPON

Voyage INDE

...ard d'Orphée"
...ici BLANCHOT
..."Elégies de Duino"
...ainer Maria RILKE
...le Théâtre de
...arionnettes" de KLEIST
...Théâtre NOH

· Coach physique pour Alain CHANFORT
· Chorégraphie pour le clip
"Les brunes comptent pas pour des prunes"
de LIO

"Judex" de
Georges Franju

...Dombrecht
..LAUWERS

Gérard POLI

Bruno Goubert

...Frère

Anne Grère
Paul Droulers

JUNKO SHIMADA

Sylvie Galein
Pierre Droulers

...na Borriello
...n Deihim
...ya SATO
...STON Tong
...e Droulers

Adriana Borriello
Pierre Droulers

Sofie

Pierre Droulers

Adriana Borriello
Pierre Droulers

Charly DEGOTTE
Pierre Droulers

"Interprète dans
"Face à Face" de
Michèle Anne De Mey
(Théâtre 140/BXL)

Valérie Castan
Antoine Effroy
Christine Gafny-Brunet
Muriel Hérault
Isabelle Le
Anne Karine Lescop
Françoise Rognerud
Pierre Rubio

Charly Degotte
Pierre Droulers

...STON TONG
...n DEIHIM

GHEDALIA TAZARTÈS
Sussan Deihim

THIERRY DE MEY

Serge PROKOFIEV

Sussan Deihim
avec Bruno Goubert
(montage sonore)

...ographie:
...GONZE

"Miserere, the reflection
...heus and Eurydice"
...é par Winston Tong

ÉRIC PAUWELS
Réalisation du
film 16mm
(Arriflex Aaton)

Frédérique LAGNY
(ass. à la dramaturgie)

...stival de
...TEAUVALLON
...RIS CWB
...al d'Été
...RQUEN

· Théâtre de La Bastille
(dir. Denise Lucioni)
· Foyer Culturel Sart-Tilman
Liège

· Ouverture de la
grand Hall
Halles de Schaerbeek
Bruxelles

les lundis de
La Balsamine
Bruxelles

· CNDC Angers
· Centre Pompidou
Paris
· La Roche/Yon

les lundis de
La Balsamine
Bruxelles

...RNATIONAL
...NIE PIERRE DROULERS (FRANCE)

...SERERE	MIDI-MINUIT	STRIPTIZ	SAMSONETTE	CADAVRE EXQUIS	Sonnettes Trotinettes
	IMPROVISATION	PALINDROME			+ Multes et Moultes
1985	1986	1987	1988	1989

Solo Danse
suite au spectacle
de dominique petit

" les œuvres d'art naissent
toujours de qui a affronté
le danger, de qui est allé
jusqu'au bout d'une
expérience, jusqu'au point
que nul humain ne peut
dépasser. Plus loin
on pousse et plus
propre plus personnelle
plus unique devient une
vie.

Rilke

PIECE OF STRING

.

OTHERNESS/AUTISM

Every time I found myself in a group situation, I was attracted by the
aspect of disturbance, difference: another culture, colour, religion,
another form of behaviour. I can't explain it, it's unconscious. Autism
is an extreme form of difference. I danced with an autist and I was very
disturbed. His reactions had nothing to do with those of another dancer.
Autists have a completely different conception of time and space. They
reformulate the question of our framework, of our personal structure.

ARRIVING/LEAVING

There is always a moment when we don't know if we are arriving or if we are
leaving! They are movements that go together, a way of being, of living.
We arrive and we leave. I've always liked this quotation from James Joyce:
'They lived and laughed and loved and left.' Often, to make something emerge,
you need to disengage. This corresponds to eastern reasoning, where creating
is subtracting. Ann Veronica Janssens works in this way. She will show that
something is already there by hollowing out a hole in space. This is an
overall obsession with transformation. To make an image appear in a work,
you need to work through many images before arriving at a finished product.

AUDITION

To audition is to listen, to be attentive, to watch. If you are receptive,
you feel someone speaking to you, even if they are not talking to you. It's
a touch of alchemy, a communication.

PINA BAUSCH

I saw two works by Pina Bausch the same year in Avignon. I was enthralled.
She was the daughter of a restaurant owner. As a child, she saw everything
hidden beneath the tables; power games, games of seduction. It was a
treasure. It's a German expressionist style. I am more on the side of
painting, of abstraction, the Americans.

HAPPINESS

One day I was in Paris, I had just cleaned the whole apartment, I opened the
window. A bird flew in and landed on the floor, shook itself in the sun, then

left. It was an outside manifestation of exactly the same thing that I had
just been doing, a fresh, open space. A perfect equation between interior
and exterior, an answer.

BRAM/AFFILIATION

Having a son. Living your own childhood again. What should we pass on? It's
not a reproduction. The nascent being is already born. The child is not
your double. But giving him an initial push so that he finds his own way.
Kahlil Gibran said: 'Your children are not your children…'

BRUSSELS/PARIS – GARE DU NORD/GARE DU MIDI

In my head I have never settled. I have often been overtaken by this desire
to go somewhere else. But I always come back to where I came from. Brussels,
with its architecture, its reliability and the feeling that it gives off,
embodies a confused and oppressive place. Paris is more sparkling, more
lively, more turbulent. Its energy is more radiant. Even if this light is
artificial, it is seductive. These two cities generate a vacillation between
light and dark, work and pleasure.

BEGINNING (AND ENDING)

In my end is my beginning.

COLOURS

Colour has a physical quality, which produces a certain energy. By painting
or through reading, I've made a study of colour. It has different meanings
depending on the culture. I was interested in working with colour on stage
to accentuate or attenuate an emotion, a feeling, to shift perceptions. Two
axioms are very important for me. Firstly, Goethe's who said something like
'Colours are the sufferings of white'. And Pierre Soulages who said that 'All
colours are contained within black'.

ANNE TERESA DE KEERSMAEKER

At one time, I stopped working as a choreographer for a while. As an actor
in *Ottone Ottone*, I discovered other ways of creating. Of writing a script.
I was interested to see how Anne Teresa maintained the sense of group in

the act of writing, with each person's ego and the question of unity in the community of sharing. I was completely confident and I was curious to see where it led. I learned from her tenacity. If you need to join in a debate on the Flemish and the Walloons, the ways of preparing for this are very different. There was a strategy. Before starting a work, Anne Teresa already had a whole series of dates in circulation. For us, a premiere was often decisive.

GARDENS

In my childhood home, there were three connecting gardens. The first with a square lawn, very well kept, with an arched gateway and a swing, the paths neatly defined. We played a lot there. We celebrated communions there. The second one was wilder, with hazelnut trees, stinging nettles and bushes. That was where we built our dens and hid tins with chocolates, cigarettes… forbidden things. The third garden was a complete mess. There was an abandoned house, with broken masonry, a collapsed attic. One day we found a German helmet. We didn't go there very often, we were frightened. These three gardens often resurface in my dreams. The first garden is consciousness, display; the second, the subconscious, an off-balance world; and the third, the unconscious, war. If we transpose this configuration to my work, *MA* would be the first garden, *Flowers* the second, and *Walk Talk Chalk* the third.

BUSTER KEATON AND COMPOSING

In *De l'air et du vent* we used a fragment from *Steamboat Bill, Jr.* and with the performers we put together a reinterpretation of the sequence: running, jumping, falling… In reproducing it like this, by following it to the letter like a score, at the end it didn't really resemble the film at all.
    Unlike Charlie Chaplin who works with tragi-comedy and emotions, Buster Keaton works with writing and the architecture of movement. With great economy of means, he finds solutions for staging. He is less interested in the psychological characters, as is Chaplin, but more interested in playing with the contrast between stage and off stage. He never laughs. He puts on a mask, doesn't pull faces. He is not far away from Japanese *no* and *kabuki*, from these more abstract traditions.

IMPROVISATION

In New York, I discovered free jazz. Free writing, a direct writing without structure, with the idea of going beyond. One day, I was dancing with Steve Lacy and I realised that we were completely in harmony, sharing the same space, the same energy. Making my way, what interested me was to improvise using starting points, substance, hindrances.

THE NAKED ISLAND

The Naked Island by Kaneto Shindo (1960) was the cult film of my parents. I saw it very young. During the whole film, the only couple who lived on this island went to the mainland to look for fresh water to water their vegetable patch. The film is just made up with this action. At a particular moment, the woman bumps into a rock, spills the water and is slapped by her husband. This slap becomes an event, an explosion, even if it is not emphasised. Afterwards we don't say anything. Life carries on.

MA

Before the creation of *MA* I read *S, M, L, XL* by Rem Koolhaas and Bruce Mau. I was interested in this question: How can an individual construct his personal mythology in an urban context? Strolling allows you to find a temporality, a speed that is suited to imagining the future. This resonates with the approach of artists: how to secure a space where we can exist as we are.

Ma in Japanese means to connect. That could be maybe a bridge, a journey between stations, a conversation: listen then speak, like the Japanese do. That could also be an accident, an interruption. In Japan, thresholds are very important. When you enter your home, you take off your shoes. You mark the limit between the town and the house. The work *MA* combines all these thresholds, all these *ma*. When the audience was arriving in the theatre foyer, they heard what was happening in the street, then once they were in the auditorium, what they heard from the foyer…

MARSEILLE

Marseille is a gateway. To Africa, to the south, the sea, the horizon. It's an hallucinating conglomerate of complexities. A multi-coloured, violent, unassailable city. It's the only city in the south of France like that. It shares with Brussels a certain relationship with chaos.

MEDITATION

Meditating is entering into delicate contact with yourself. Getting friendly with your spirit in order to be able to travel with it without any more struggling, getting into conflicts, and resistance. Working with all the emotions that flow through us. It's training the spirit. You feel a physicality, you dance with your emotions. To that effect, you need to accept everything: ugliness, misery, beauty, grace. Reacting calmly to everything that presents itself. Meditation provides compassion, which allows to recognise in the suffering of others a part of yourself. It's not easy. You need to be attuned to your fundamental instincts and their ramifications. You think that meditation will calm you down, allow you to retire to a quiet place. It's not the case.

WHITE BLACKBIRD

When we put on *Multum in Parvo*, there was a door at the back of the theatre that opened on to a wild garden. I opened the door two-thirds of the way through the performance, and after a few moments, we heard a blackbird singing. The whole audience heard it. There is no better singer than a blackbird. It was the flip side of the performance. A reality that found itself being staged. An ordinary thing that became extraordinary, exceptional.

THE NORTH SEA

When we say 'Let's go to the seaside', we immediately think of space, of a clear horizon and your body becomes infected and affected by the feeling. You open up into space. Westende, that means the end of the West, and Ostende, the end of the East. As a child, I often made the journey between them on a *cuistax*, the small tricycle that you can hire on the seafront. The North Sea is rather like a wall: it's a sea that strangely doesn't lead to islands or to an elsewhere. It's like an ending. On the Belgian coast, the sky, the earth and the sea are often the same colour. They merge one into the other. I often find that soothing.

ORPHEUS AND EURYDICE

Orpheus, he who travels to the other side, looking for the inspirational figure (Eurydice). He doesn't write, he sings and he dances. The menace of death is a boundary. To cross over, you need to give as good as you get.

STEVE PAXTON

Steve Paxton and Lisa Nelson used to come to my studio. They performed improvisations with objects that were there. As I found this interesting, I suggested an improvisation showing them what I could do with these objects. They watched me and said that they would have another go. This time Steve Paxton followed what I did more closely. That could seem not very creative. But he made me understand the contrary. Creativity consists of carefully watching something and, using its subjectivity and its body, making something else.

STAGE

What I like most is arriving in a theatre with nobody there and seeing the empty stage. There, we find all the metaphysics of space waiting for action. The space is empty at the beginning of dreams. Like in a street, when a house or building is destroyed. The empty space fills up with possibilities. That's also the case after a performance.

PRESENCE

You can't make presence. I remember the beginning of *Trois voyageurs regardent un lever de soleil*, directed by Claude Régy. We were immersed in a very subtle perception. There was very little action. Time was protracted. For twenty minutes the four characters were walking very slowly, like a body swaying from right to left. After twenty minutes, Michael Lonsdale, with his unique voice, said: 'But I am happy to see the sunrise again.' Through the environment in which Claude Régy had placed us, that became a happening, thought in motion.

PUNK AND POGO

Le Gibus, in Paris, in the 1980s. Heartbreakers concert. Lots of people and energy gathered in a limited space. It's pulsating, everybody jumping up and down at the same time. We bang into each other. It's not bad. So we up the pace. Stimulating each other. I remember Johnny Rotten coming on stage at the Théâtre 140. It was electric.

RITUALS

I share James Joyce's thought that says that 'rituals are the artist's resting place'. I have rituals. For example, if I meet someone I won't say anything straightaway. First of all, I will mark time and watch him, then I will start the conversation. Marking the moment, in order to allow communication with him. Or even doing the washing-up. It goes far. I was struck by this story of a disciple who asked: 'Master, what is illumination?' He replies: 'Have you finished eating?' – 'Yes.' – 'So go and wash up your bowl.' If you are completely immersed in what you do, you are well. When you are not very well is when you are present but you are elsewhere, that you are doing something else. Doing the washing-up is not very creative, compared to cooking when you need to at least think about the pinch of salt. It's like an empty stage. Ritual is to stop. That happens to me sometimes in the street. I stop, I look at what is happening around me and a space opens up… It's a question of presence, also with the idea of having a rest from swirling, exhausting thoughts.

TASK

In *Mountain/Fountain*, taken from *Conte Mikkaddo* by Michel François, it was necessary to find an order for organising the objects that worked. That coincided with some information on the notion of *task* that I had just received from Trisha Brown. The *task* was a thing to do independently of idea or feeling. It was linked to another concept, that of *score*. Instead of creating out of nothing, we simply created a choreography by choosing a framework and by concentrating on the analysis of this framework, its substance, its form, its qualities. This data was used for the score and was transformed into gesture. The body processed the known information and made it into something else. I had chosen as an exercise, as a *task*, the paper folded into four. I bent my body into two, then into four, and I found the solutions to problems that emerged later. During this stage, we observed that each subjectivity remade the same *task* differently.

CHÖGYAM TRUNGPA

Chögyam Trungpa is a Tibetan master who has come to the West to teach. I was interested in his wisdom, which was in reality a 'mad wisdom', as he puts it. In my Christian culture, wisdom consists of calming down personal madness, eccentricities, mollifying, smoothing, being well-behaved. Except

there is no wisdom without madness. Wisdom is not a fixed state that we can
separate out from something else. It comforts subjectivity, singularity.
It's having to have a bit of a crazy game with the world. Live your
differences to the point where this becomes wisdom. Shamans have this power
of eccentricity. They prepare their trances, practise for them. They are
accepted, and acknowledged by the community, even in their madness. And in
turn they reinforce the community.

GIAMBATTISTA VICO

Through Joyce, I discovered Vico's thoughts. The spring that becomes a
stream, which merges into other rivers, transforms into an estuary, flows
into the sea, dissolves into clouds and falls as rain, to become a spring.
Of this great cycle, Joyce spoke of human life. I like the combination of
this abstraction with very concrete things.

JOURNEYS

You can travel in your bedroom or on the spot, it's very difficult,
but it's possible. Gilles Deleuze doesn't travel but talks a lot about
deterritorialisation and geography. The inward journey, feeling, moving,
that's the real journey, the way in which you perceive the world, things.
We are always travelling. Take a journey into space, that could be a
development. Going to Japan, to Brazil. Experiencing feelings, intensifying
them. Going on a journey with one's own mad wisdom.

Compileded by Fabienne Aucant, December 2016, Brussels.

.

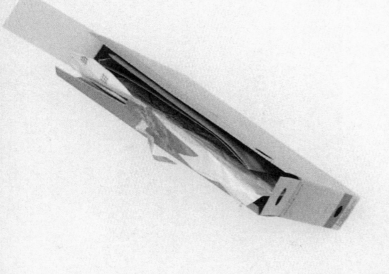

BE A
POEM

BE A
POEM

2010

BEING BEAUTEO

CONTRIBUTORS & IMAGES

JEAN-MARC ADOLPHE
Jean-Marc Adolphe, born in 1958, journalist and essayist, founded and directed the magazine *Mouvement* from 1993 to 2014. He is the author of numerous works about dance, theatre and the politics of culture. As artistic advisor, he worked for the Théâtre de la Bastille, Paris, from 1994 to 2001, and then at the Espace des Arts, Scène Nationale, at Chalon-sur-Saône, from 2002 to 2007.

FABIENNE AUCANT
Fabienne Aucant, born in 1974, worked for ten years at the Halles de Schaerbeek, Brussels, in particular as the curator of a series of poetry-performances, of meetings, lectures and symposiums on the questions of artistic and political engagement. In 2009 she joined the *centre chorégraphique* of Charleroi Danses for the production and performance of Pierre Droulers work, to accompany young choreographers, and to develop artistic projects at La Raffinerie.

TARQUIN BILLIET
Tarquin Billiet, born in 1960, has worked in a variety of different cultural fields: after three years as assistant administrative director at Charleroi Danses, he was artistic director of Brussels' Flagey cultural centre, then of the *Festival Ars Musica*, followed by general secretary of Opéra de Lille. He is currently director of Artistic Transversal Projects at Bozar, Brussels. After an initial collaboration between 1993 and 1995, he has often worked in various roles with Pierre Droulers.

MALIKA DJARDI
Malika Djardi, born in 1985, was trained in the visual arts, before joining the University of Quebec in Montreal and then the Centre National de Danse Contemporaine in Angers from 2009 to 2011. With her solo work *Sa prière*, created as part of the *Danseur* festival in Brussels in April 2014, she continued her research into the question of performance as an object of documentation. Her second creation, the duo *Horion*, was presented as part of *Rencontres Chorégraphiques Internationales de Seine-Saint-Denis* in 2016. Since 2011 she has worked as a performer for Mélanie Perrier, Pierre Droulers, Joris Lacoste, Ola Maciejewska, Clyde Chabot, Alexandre Roccoli…

MICHEL FRANÇOIS
Michel François, born in 1956, is a visual artist. His exhibitions include: documenta 9 at Kassel, 1992; Witte de With, Rotterdam, 1997; Kunsthalle, Berne, 1999; Venice Biennale, 1999, with A.V. Janssens; Haus der Kunst, Munich, 2000; Artpace, San Antonio, Texas, 2004; SMAK, Ghent, 2009; IAC, Villeurbanne, 2010; Mac's, Grand-Hornu, 2012; Crac, Sète, 2012; Ikon Gallery, Birmingham, 2014; *Take the Floor*, KVS, Brussels/Théâtre de la Cité internationale, Paris, 2015; *Tierra Vaga*, Fundación Casa Wabi, Puerto Escondido (Mexico), 2016; « The Absent Museum », WIELS, Brussels, 2017.

YVES-NOËL GENOD
Yves-Noël Genod, born in 1972, has always acted and directed. His first work was with with Claude Régy and François Tanguy. Beginning with the discipline of improvised contact, he gravitated towards dance, his main collaboration being with Loïc Touzé. In 2003 the choreographer suggested that Genod put together his first performance, entitled *En attendant Genod*, which was based on the model of English stand-up comedy. This was followed by commissions (where he was always given carte blanche), shows (more than sixty to date) and performances mostly as part of festivals, in dance venues or in hybrid forms – theatrical performances in which drama and action have been removed, leaving only poetry and ghostly presences.

YVES GODIN
Yves Godin, born in 1962, has been a creative lighting engineer since the beginning of the 1990s, essentially for dance, then for performance, visual arts, theatre and music. Today Godin mainly works on lighting and staging, with Boris Charmatz, Olivia Grandville, Pascal Rambert, Vincent Dupont and Thierry Balasse. He collaborated with Pierre Droulers in the creation of *Flowers* in 2007 and *Walk Talk Chalk* in 2009. In parallel with his stage work he creates installations and events on and around the subject of light.

GRAND MAGASIN
Grand Magasin was founded by Pascale Murtin and François Hiffler in 1982. Under this name, together they have conceived over forty performances, smaller pieces and presentations, involving, when appropriate, the services of their friends (such as Bettina Atala from 2001 to 2010) for the pleasure of varying their formats and line-ups. Brandishing the slogan 'rare and cheap', Grand Magasin have over time put on many public gatherings, stage happenings, art gallery performances and open-air events.

MANON GREINER
Manon Greiner, born in 1982 in West Berlin, began learning classical ballet, the piano and violin very early. Selected for the biannual programme D.A.N.C.E (Dance Apprentice Network aCross Europe) directed by William Forsythe, Wayne

McGregor, Frédéric Flamand and Angelin Preljocaj, in 2007 she obtained her Master's Degree in Dance at the Palucca School of Dance in Dresden. She has worked with La Fura dels Baus, Michèle Anne De Mey, Thierry De Mey, William Forsythe, Angelin Preljocaj, Lutz Gregor, Pierre Droulers, Wayne McGregor, Prue Lang, Jasper Džuki Jelen, Ezequiel Sanucci, Chuo-Tai Sun, Ceso Gelabert, Morgan Belenguer, Jean-Guillaume Weis… In 2013 she re-joined the Scottish Dance Theatre, performing the repertoires of Victor Quijada and Jo Strømgren, and working with Fleur Darkin, Jorge Crecis and Damien Jalet.

HAROLD HENNING
Harold Henning, born in 1976, is a performer and creator for the theatre, dance and circus. He began his career in 1997 as a performer for Pierre Droulers (*Mountain/Fountain*, *Multum in Parvo*, *Ma*, *Aventures/Nouvelles Aventures*, *Carte Blanche*, *Agora*). Since then he has collaborated with several Belgian artists and groups, including Les Ballets C. de la B., Miet Warlop, Mauro Paccagnella, Cie Mossoux-Bonté… and in particular with Cie SOIT/Hans Van den Broeck. He is co-founder of the theatre company Clinic Orgasm Society. In 2006 he created and played in the duo *Leopoldo* (with Mohamed Benaji, alias Ben Fury), and has subsequently developed his own work (*Stay On the Scene*, 2013; *L'oeil nu*, 2016; *The Old Loop*, 2017).

ANN VERONICA JANSSENS
Ann Veronica Janssens, born in 1956, has, since the end of the 1970s, put together an experimental oeuvre that consists principally of on-site installations using very simple materials or even immaterial constituents such as light, sound or artificial fog. The viewer is confronted with the idea of the 'unattainable' and with a fleeting experience where he goes beyond the threshold of a clear and controlled vision. It's an experience of loss of control, of instability, of fragility, whether it be visual, physical, temporal or psychological.

DENISE LUCCIONI
Denise Luccioni, born in 1951, discovered an artistic world through John Cage and the Judson Church at the Fêtes Musicales de la Sainte-Baume (1970s). She then focused on choreographic and theatrical creativity; distribution, production, programming, writing, visual lectures… working with Bénédicte Pesle's Artservice International and of founding the Cinémathèque de la danse and programming at the Théâtre de la Bastille. She also launched the *Soirées nomades* at the Fondation Cartier, translated books about dance and theatrical works and wrote essays about cinema. As much as creating things herself, she makes them known, makes them exist and be loved – and she is the witness.

BARBARA MANZETTI
Barbara Manzetti, born in 1970, in Rome, is a choreographer and author.

DENIS MARIOTTE
Denis Mariotte, born in 1961, is a composer, musician, performer and visual artist. Since 1990 he has collaborated with Maguy Marin on over twenty performances, putting together all sorts of creative soundtracks: music performed on stage, electro-acoustic recordings, vocal works, sound arrangements and film music. Simultaneously, he has worked as a musician with Fred Frith on the works *Impur* and *Stick Figures* in 1998. As a duo, he has created very hybrid pieces with Maguy Marin and with Renaud Golo. He has also composed several solo pieces, including work that unites music and movement in a mobile physical composition. From 2013 onwards, he has been exploring new ways of working, which are closer to installation.

EUGÈNE SAVITZKAYA
Eugène Savitzkaya, born in 1955, lives in Belgium, has been feasting in the French style (following the model of Jude Stefan) since 1972. He has published novels, plays and poetry, and has worked in the cinema, in architecture and town planning. Has no intention of stopping soon. Tends to prefer the asthenosphere.

HANS THEYS
Hans Theys, born in 1963, is the author of around thirty books and several hundred interviews and essays on contemporary art. As curator he has organised over forty exhibitions. He is in charge of teaching at the Royal Academy in Antwerp and at the Academy of Ghent (KASK).

Cover   *Désert*, Pierre Droulers, Plan K, Brussels 1979

     Pierre Droulers, with two horses, northern France, 1960

p.2   Bram Droulers in *1er Avril* by Yves-Noël Genod, La Raffinerie, Brussels, 2011

p. 4   Pierre Droulers in New York, 1977

p. 13   *Dispersion*, Pierre Droulers, Théâtre de Poche, Brussels, 1977

p. 15   *Hedges* tour, Fontevraud Abbey, 1980

p. 17   Anna and Robert Droulers (Pierre's parents) in the studio, during a 'Monday evenings' gathering, Lambersart, 1950s

p. 19   Pierre Droulers on a *ouistax* in Westende, 1950s

pp. 20-21 Table, 'Connections' © Yvan Guerdon

p. 22   Maurice Béjart, 1978 © Colette Masson

p.23   Pierre Droulers in *Le Fils de l'air* by Maurice Béjart, Cirque royal, Brussels, 1972 © Claire Falcy

pp. 24-25 Juliana Carneiro da Cunha and Maguy Marin, Place du Jeu de Balle, Brussels, 1971 © Stéphane Lagasse, © 2017 Sofam

pp. 26-27 Pierre Droulers in a play by Alain Louafi, Mudra, Brussels, 1972 © Claire Falcy

p. 28   Danielle Cousins, *Opening Blues*, extract from *Désert*, Brussels, 1976.

p. 29   Punk concert by Peet and Ses Rats, Pierre Droulers at the microphone, Île d'Yeu, 1970s

pp. 30-31 Landing stage in Île d'Yeu, 1970s © Pierre Droulers

p. 32   Leaflet for *The Penny Arcade Peep Show*, directed by Frédéric Flamand, Brussels, 1975

p. 33   *Désert*, Juliana Carneiro da Cunha, Jean Gaudin and Jean-Christophe Lamy, Mudra, Brussels, 1972

pp. 34-35 *Désert*, Juliana Carneiro da Cunha and Pierre Droulers, Mudra, Brussels, 1972

p. 37   New York, 1977 © Pierre Droulers

pp. 38-39 Table, 'New York' © Yvan Guerdon

p. 40   Johnny Rotten, passport pic, 1977 © John Lydon

p. 41   Arthur Rimbaud © Etienne Carjat

p. 42   Public Image Ltd, 'Religion', from *First Issue*, Virgin label, London, 1978.

p. 43   Arthur Rimbaud, 'Matin', from *Une saison en enfer*, Paris, 1873.

p. 44   A friend, Flavienne, Brussels, 1970s © Pierre Droulers

p. 45   Another friend, Isabelle, Brussels, 1970s

p. 46   Poem by Chiaro Teatrino, published Nuovi Strumenti

p. 47   Pierre Droulers in New York, 1977

p. 48   Jerzy Grotowski, 1973 © Aleksander Jalosinki

p. 49   Robert Wilson in front af the theater © Allan Tannenbaum, Getty Images

pp. 50-51 Art Ensemble of Chicago, *Nice Guys*, record sleeve, ECM, 1979 © Isio Saba

p. 53   Steve Paxton and Carolyn Brown in *Aeon* by Merce Cunningham, New York, 1961 © Richard Rutledge

p. 54   Sheryl Sutton in *Le Regard du sourd* by Robert Wilson, Paris, 1971 © Ivan Farkas

p. 55   Steve Lacy, 1980s © Hozumi Nakadaira

p. 57   Steve Lacy and Pierre Droulers, Plan K, Brussels, 1979 © Stéphane Lagasse, © 2017 Sofam

pp. 58-59 Table, 'Brussels-Paris' © Yvan Guerdon

pp. 60-61 *Hedges*, Pierre Droulers, Plan K, Brussels, 1979 © Hubert Dombrecht

pp. 62-63 *Hedges*, Pierre Droulers, Plan K, Brussels, 1979

p. 64   Gare du Midi, Brussels, 1970s © Stéphane Lagasse, © 2017 Sofam

p. 65   Gare du Nord, Paris, 2015 © Pierre Droulers

p. 66   Party in Paris, 1980

p. 67   Party in Paris, 1980

pp. 68-69 Party in Paris, 1980 © Simon Boca Negra

p. 70   Poster by Michel François for the project *Appartement à louer*, Brussels, 1980 © Michel François

p. 71   Ann Veronica Janssens, party, Brussels, 1980 © Pierre Droulers

p. 73   Sheryl Sutton and Pierre Droulers, Paris 1980

pp. 74-75 Sheryl Sutton, *Fall*, experimenting in the studio, Paris, 1980

pp. 76-77 *Tao*, Pierre Droulers and Sheryl Sutton, Centre Wallonie-Bruxelles, Paris, 1980

p. 79   François Hiffler et Pascale Murtin, Grand Magasin © Véronique Schiltz

pp. 80-81 Table, 'Brothers & Sisters' © Yvan Guerdon

p. 82   Pierre Droulers and François Hiffler rehearsing *Tips*, Plan K, Brussels, 1981 © Marc Trivier, © 2017 Sofam

p. 83   The legs of Pascale Murtin and François Hiffler thrusting out of the car window, Ostend, 1981 © Pierre Droulers

p. 84   Arthur Rimbaud, 'Royauté', from *Illuminations*, Paris, 1895.

p. 84   The DS belonging to Minimal Compact, 1982

p. 85   Minimal Compact (Malka Spigel, Samy Birnbach and Berry Sakharof), Brussels, 1982 © Crammed Discs,

     photo: Charles Von Hoorick

p. 86   Minimal Compact, *Made to Measure Vol. 1*, CD case, Crammed Discs, 1984

pp. 86-87 *Pieces for Nothing*, Pierre Droulers and Malka Spigel, improvisation, Brussels, 1982

pp. 88-89 *Hedges* tour, Pierre Droulers, Steve Lacy and Eric Sleichim, Pisa, 1982 © Annie Trezel

p. 90   *Hedges* tour, Pierre Droulers in the gardens, Pisa, 1982 © Annie Trezel

p. 91   *Hedges* tour, Pierre Droulers, in the gardens, Pisa, 1982 © Annie Trezel

pp. 92-93 A friend, Grazia, in a bar in Filicudi, Italy, 1981 © Pierre Droulers

pp. 94-95 Beach with parasols, Cagliari, Sardinia, 1983 © Pierre Droulers

pp. 96-97 Nude on the rocks, Corsica, 1983 © Pierre Droulers

p. 99   *La Jetée*, Patrick Beckers, Pierre Droulers and *ouistax* wheel, Plan K, Brussels, 1983 © Elian Bachini

pp. 100-01 Table, 'Blues Black' © Yvan Guerdon

pp. 102-03 Solitude, unknown person on a boat, 1984 © Pierre Droulers

p. 104   The pier at Port-Joinville, Île d'Yeu, 1980 © Pierre Droulers

pp. 106-07 Café terrace in Ostend, 1970 © Stéphane Lagasse, © 2017 Sofam

p. 109   *La Jetée*, Eric Sleichim, Sheryl Sutton, Michèle Noiret, Pierre Droulers, Patrick Beckers, Plan K, Brussels, 1983

p. 111   Pierre Droulers in his father's studio, Saint-Rémy-de-Provence, 1983 © Patrick Bensard

pp.112-13 *Miserere*, Sussan Deyhim, Centre Wallonie-Bruxelles, Paris, 1984 © Philippe Valéra

SUNDAY. PIERRE DROULERS CHOREOGRAPHER

PUBLISHER
Mercatorfonds (Managing Director, Bernard Steyaert)
Charleroi Danses (Director, Annie Bozzini)

EDITED BY
Pierre Droulers

ASSISTED BY
Fabienne Aucant, Arnaud Meuleman

CONSULTING EDITORS
Jean-Marc Adolphe, Sofie Kokaj

CONTRIBUTIONS BY
Jean-Marc Adolphe, Fabienne Aucant, Tarquin Billiet, Malika
Djardi, Pierre Droulers, Michel François, Yves-Noël Genod,
Yves Godin, Manon Grenier, Harold Henning, François Hiffler
& Pascale Murtin, Ann Veronica Janssens, Denise Luccioni,
Barbara Manzetti, Denis Mariotte, Arnaud Meuleman, Kazuya
Sato, Eugène Savitzkaya, Hans Theys

COORDINATION
Fabienne Aucant, Charleroi Danses
Wivine de Traux, Mercatorfonds

PRODUCTION
Charleroi Danses

TRANSLATION (FROM FRENCH)
Michael Abbott

EDITING
Lise Connellan

BOOK DESIGN AND CONCEPT
Ousseynou Salla
Assistant, Jean Reynaud

FONT
Droulers by Bureau Brut

PAPER
Printed on Amber Graphic 90 g/m²

PRE-PRESS
T'Ink studio, Brussels
Riso Presto, Paris

PRINTING AND BINDING
Albe De Cooker, Antwerp

© 2017 Mercatorfonds, Brussels; Charleroi Danses, Charleroi
and Brussels; and the authors

Distributed in Belgium, the Netherlands and Luxembourg by
Mercatorfonds, Brussels
ISBN 978-94-6230-178-8
D/2017/703/21
www.mercatorfonds.be

Distributed outside Belgium, the Netherlands and Luxembourg
by Yale University Press, New Haven and London
www.yalebooks.com/art - www.yalebooks.co.uk
ISBN 978-0-300-23026-0
Library of Congress Control Number: 2017940020

Charleroi Danses is supported by the Fédération Wallonie-
Bruxelles and the city of Charleroi.
www.charleroi-danses.be

ACKNOWLEDGEMENTS

I would like to thank Arnaud Meuleman and Fabienne Aucant
without whom this book would never have happened.
I would like to thank the Charleroi Danses organisation,
represented by Vincent Thirion and then by Annie Bozzini,
who managed the interim period so that this work could be
completed.
I would like to thank Bernard Steyaert and Wivine de Traux
at Mercatorfonds for their warm welcome.
I would like to thank Marion Rhéty and Caroline Vermeulen
who began the preparation of this book, and to those who
followed its progress.
I would like to thank my travelling companions who helped to
create, produce and stage the performances that have defined
the journey.
I would like to thank all the people who have come together
to develop ways of thinking, of action and of love.
I would like to thank the performers who have disturbed me,
been ahead of me, surpassed me, as they should do.
I would like to thank nature where day still follows night.
I would like to thank Heloïse Berns for her daily support.
I would like to thank the readers who browse through this
book and I hope they find something that moves them.

Pierre Droulers

sun
day